SQL Made Easy

The Ultimate Guide for Beginners on Data Querying, Manipulation, and Analysis Using Real-World Context to Advance Your Career in Data Analytics

Alex Wade

Contents

Introduction

In a time when we're generating an incredible amount of data every day, the need for better tools to manage this data has never been more important. Structured Query Language (SQL) is the ideal language to learn for this purpose, enabling you to work easily with large amounts of data. The language was "first developed by IBM in the 1970s to allow access to databases using an easy-to-learn, English-like language. It was quickly adopted by other software vendors and soon became the industry standard for working with relational databases" (Thornhill, 2022). Even as time went by, it remained the go-to language for extracting data and maintaining databases efficiently.

Even with all the advances in technology we have today, major technology companies such as Google, Facebook, and Uber still use SQL in their systems, and it was considered the third most-used technology in 2022 (Thornhill, 2022). Because it is such a simple and easy-to-understand language, it is the perfect place to start learning if you do not have an IT background and are looking for a career change. By learning how to use SQL, you will see that many opportunities in the market will open up to you even if you have a basic understanding.

On the other hand, if you are already an IT professional that works with another coding language, you will see that by learning SQL you will discover that it adds value to your coding skills, especially when dealing with large amounts of data. Its ability to transform, extract, and interact with databases will enhance your skills and make them even more attractive to future employers. It does not matter if you are a business analyst, a software developer or architect, or a data analyst—knowing SQL will add to your skill set and enable you to find more attractive opportunities.

As you embark on your SQL journey, you will find these key benefits waiting for you:

- data consistency and integrity
- tools for data recovery and backup for system failures
- efficient and time-tested data operations
- user-friendly language
- no prior coding knowledge required

You might be wondering if this means there are no challenges at all for the beginner who is starting to work with the language. No, not at all. Learning SQL can come with some challenges that you might need to overcome. One of the most commonly mentioned among professionals is the lack of a user-friendly interface and its increasing complexity as you start dealing with more data and queries. In addition to this, there is the fact that there are two different types of SQL: ANSI SQL, which is the most common version used, and ISO SQL, which is based on an international standard. While they both have similarities, you might find some variations between the two versions.

Nevertheless, these should not be impediments to your learning process and ability to start working with SQL. In fact, as you read this book, you will be given all the information you will need to give you a great start in the language or to enhance the skills you already have. For those who are beginning, you are going to learn about the basic techniques and structures you must know to thrive when using the language. If you are already a seasoned professional looking to increase your abilities, you will also benefit from the content in this book, not only because you are going to refresh some concepts, but you will also be given some intermediate and advanced techniques as well.

This will be one of the main differences you will find in this book when compared to the other resources available online—you will learn what you need to know and be shown how to do it straightforwardly. As you read, some exercises will be proposed to test what you have learned and help fixate on the concepts that were taught in each chapter. By doing this, you will see that SQL syntax and operations will soon become second nature to you. Finally, at the end of the book, you will get to work on a real-world portfolio project, preparing you to display in the market your new skill.

As the book progresses, you will encounter exercises designed to test your knowledge and reinforce the concepts introduced in each chapter. Through these exercises, SQL syntax and operations will naturally become second nature, enabling you to work with queries independently and instinctively. Think about the wide range of opportunities that will open up: transitioning to a new career, acquiring a valuable skill, enhancing existing coding abilities, negotiating for a raise, pursuing higher-paying job opportunities, and even contributing to data-driven decision-making in your organization. In essence, by engaging with the topics covered in this book, you will gain the fluency in SQL necessary to thrive in your career.

Therefore, if you are ready to embark on a journey of acquiring essential skills and reshaping the trajectory of your career, you should continue reading! It will provide comprehensive resources to ensure a successful start or skill refinement. Join me in this educational adventure of mastering SQL, and witness how it transforms your future!

Chapter 1
Data and SQL

To understand the importance of learning SQL, we must first understand where it is used and why. If you think about the amount of information that is generated daily, organizations must find alternatives to structure and organize this data in a manner that is easily accessible and comprehensible. In addition to this, the need for finding solutions that are cost-effective in the long run and that support the organizations' needs for speed and accessibility makes SQL an interesting alternative in the market.

One of the advantages of using SQL is that it is easily available in several cloud storage services such as Microsoft Azure, AWS, and Google Cloud. Although this service is offered at an hourly rate, the cost is relatively lower than when you compare to tableless methodologies, which are charged on a pay-per-use system. While the second alternative might seem like a good option, if the data in your tableless system is not structured, it can lead to more use time and consequently, a significantly higher bill to pay (Wesley, 2023).

However, before we start looking further into the uses, advantages, and disadvantages of SQL in the market, it is essential that we take a step back and understand the bigger picture. For this reason, in this first chapter, you are going to learn the basic principles related to SQL: what data is, what databases are, types of databases, and why SQL should be considered as an option in comparison to more modern languages such as Python and R. Learning what these are, and their differences will give you the necessary foundation to understand other concepts that will be explained further along in the book. Lastly, and perhaps most importantly, this information will be essential to help you make an informed decision regarding your choice to learn and use SQL.

What Is Data?

Suppose you are in the supermarket, shopping according to a grocery list you wrote up the day before. Everything you have written on this list is data, or units that without being placed together or without context have no meaning. Once you have them organized in a list that makes sense to you and refers to the items you need, it will become information, since it is going to carry a logical meaning. While in this example I have used a grocery list to illustrate the concept, data can refer to practically any fact or unit, such as numbers, files, symbols, graphs, images, texts, observations, and so much more.

This means that if you have a list of numbers on a paper without explaining what they are, you will have data. However, if you say that these are the heights of all the children in a classroom, you will be giving it context and it will become information. When we transfer this representation to a business, it is possible to understand why data is so important: It will be the list of clients, prices, access to the website, purchases made, billing addresses, and everything that the business needs to function efficiently.

But what happens if this data is not cleaned and organized, and the business cannot work or draw conclusions from it? This means that it will be useless, and you will not be able to transform it into relevant information from which conclusions can be extracted. For this reason, most companies choose to organize this data into a *database*, where it will be collected and stored in an organized manner.

Each organization will structure their databases according to their needs and type of business. This means that not all databases are the same. In fact, if you think about the different types of databases available in the market, you will see there are many types to choose from. There are specific databases used for objects and others used for graphs, those used for operations, and also for personal information. In addition to this, we also have centralized, distributed, on-the-cloud, and on-premises. For this book, we are going to focus on one specific type, which is also the most popular: the relational database.

Relational Databases

A relational database can also be considered a table since the data is organized into rows and columns. This data is going to be spread across different tables, which will have one unique common identifier that will connect the information between all of them. "Analysts use SQL queries to combine different data points and summarize business performance, allowing organizations to gain insights, optimize workflows, and identify new opportunities" (IBM, 2023).

Let's suppose you are going to create a database with data on the students in one class. You are going to have the name of the student and, in each table, the grades pertaining to a certain discipline such as math, science, English, social studies, physical education, arts, and music. While each of these tables will have different numbers according to the student's performance in the discipline, they can all be connected because you have the unique identifier which is the student's name, which can be found in all tables. This means that if you're a teacher and need to discuss a student's progress with their parents, you can easily retrieve all their grades from the relational database by simply searching for their name.

All relational databases have four characteristics that enable transactions to be carried out efficiently. These are represented by the acronym ACID, which, according to IBM (2023), can be defined as follows:

- **Atomicity:** All changes to data are performed as if they are a single operation. That is, all the changes are performed, or none of them are.
- **Consistency:** Data remains in a consistent state from state to finish, reinforcing data integrity.
- **Isolation:** The intermediate state of a transaction is not visible to other transactions, and as a result, transactions that run concurrently appear to be serialized.
- **Durability:** After the successful completion of a transaction, changes to data persist and are not undone, even in the event of a system failure.

However, despite all these characteristics, you might be wondering how this information is managed and what enables the queries to be carried out. This management process is carried out by a specific software called the relational database management system (RDBMS), which enables the users to access, store, modify, structure, and organize the data within their tables as well as perform queries. Essentially speaking, the RDBMS is the interface the user will have to access and manage the data. Some popular examples include SQLite, Oracle, MySQL, PostgreSQL, Microsoft SQL Server, and MariaDB.

Relational vs. Nonrelational Databases

Although relational databases are the most commonly found structures in organizations, there is a counterpart to it known as a nonrelational database. The main difference between them is how the data is stored: While the relational database will have the data organized in tables, the nonrelational database stores the information in a nontabular form. "Non-relational databases are sometimes referred to as 'NoSQL,' which stands for Not Only SQL" (MongoDB, n.d.). Here is an example of how the data would be stored in each of these different databases:

Relational Database

Student Name	Science Grade
John	A
Mary	B
Sam	B+

Nonrelational Database

Student first name: John
Student last name: Smith
Address: 1234, Pacific Drive
City: Summerset
Birthdate: 02/28/1994
Teacher name: Mary Jones

As you can see, both of these databases store data, but the way they will be accessed and organized will differ, especially in structure. One of the advantages of a nonrelational database when compared to a relational one is that the first will allow you to handle data faster, since it has fewer tables to extract the information from, making the process more dynamic. However, there is a reason (in fact, a few) as to why relational databases are more commonly used in the market, and we are going to look at what they are now.

Benefits of Relational Databases

The first advantage of using relational databases can be seen when you analyze the structure they use to store the data. It is a straight-forward approach that does not require complex designs or a specific architecture. However, this simplicity does not mean these databases have a rigid structure that does not enable changes. On the contrary, relational databases are flexible and allow the size of the database to be easily up or downscaled according to the needs. "A data analyst can insert, update or delete tables, columns, or individual data in the given database system promptly and effi-ciently, to meet the business needs" (Pedamkar, 2023).

In addition to the flexibility and the scaling possibilities the rela-tional database offers the user, another advantage is the easy access to data while still maintaining its integrity. This is because when exploring the data in a relational database, queries can be carried out by any person who has SQL knowledge. Furthermore, because the data is organized into specific and targeted fields of the table, it is easier to establish a relationship between the different records contained in the tables, ensuring results with more precision and reliability.

How Do Relational Databases and SQL Work Together?

When considering the relationship between relational databases and SQL, there are a few analogies that can be made that will make the understanding clearer. Let's look back into the example of the school database, in which each discipline has a list of the students in the class and their grades. When the report cards are going to be generated, the user will need to give the system a command to retrieve the information based on the unique criteria that is contained in all the tables. In this case, if you remember well, we are talking about the student's name. This means that a command in SQL will be given to search for each of the students' names and bring back all the registered grades in the database for that unique identifier.

But there are other circumstances in which this can be applied. Think about a library. There, you will have different books (data) that are organized into different sections (tables) based on their theme. You will have romance, suspense, medicine, and science, to name a few random examples. Now, to search for the book you want, you need a system, or it will be impossible to find what you are looking for. To solve this, the library offers a catalog, in which you can search for each book based on their different characteristics. In this example, the catalog system would be the SQL or the means that you will use to retrieve the information and find the book you want. However, in this structure, the information contained is more complex, since each book has different characteristics they can be identified by, such as author, number of pages, category, and even publication language.

To put it simply, SQL is going to be the tool you will use to make sense of all the data contained in the database. It will help you manage and manipulate the data, making it understandable and enabling conclusions to be drawn from it.

What Is SQL?

As you already know, SQL is short for Structured Query Language, and it was developed in 1974 as an easy way to retrieve information from relational databases, which were created a few years prior, in 1970. The language was initially created by IBM specialists, and "became a standard of the American National Standards Institute (ANSI) in 1986, and the International Organization for Standardization (ISO) in 1987" (Tutorials Point, 2019). As such, SQL and its different dialects are the standard used when working with data queries in RDBMS.

When managing relational databases, SQL enables you to filter, select, group, join, and sort data according to your needs. These characteristics make it a versatile option for those working with databases of different sizes, ranging from small to big, and to help organize the information in a way that it can be understood and analyzed. Furthermore, it presents one significant advantage when compared to other languages: It is a standard simple to use and understand, and requires no previous coding experience.

But you might be wondering if there are other advantages in learning SQL, or even if there are any disadvantages at all for its use. To better understand what makes it such a popular language despite its shortcomings, let's take a look into the main characteristics that attract developers to work with SQL and its best applications.

SQL Advantages and Disadvantages

To better illustrate the advantages and disadvantages of learning and using SQL, here is a table that summarizes its main characteristics:

Advantages	Disadvantages
Interactive language	Complicated interface
Standardized language	Costly
Simple and user-friendly	Less flexibility than NoSQL
Data consistency	Complexity in structure and management
Data integrity	Partial control
Data security	Constant threats of security breaches
Scalable	Limited performance for larger datasets
Fast query processing	Lack of real-time analytics
Portable	Increased storage needs

As you can see, there is a balance between its advantages and disadvantages, although if you look closely, you will identify that the disadvantages will depend on how the relational database is used. It is because of some of these limitations that some professionals, such as data scientists and engineers, business analysts, and others who work with data sometimes opt for a different and more versatile language, such as Python and R. However, are they really the best option? Read on to find out!

SQL vs...

When we are talking about managing data, it has become commonplace that the first languages that come to mind are Python or R. This is because several companies have incorporated them into their systems, and also because they offer some benefits when compared to SQL. However, SQL wouldn't be alive for so long if it didn't have its own advantages when compared to these more modern languages.

Many people who are just starting their data journey often have doubts about what language to use and which one to learn. To ensure that you are aware of the differences and have sufficient knowledge to make an informed decision, in this final section of the chapter, you are going to learn more about the characteristics of each of these. A comparison will be made between all three languages, and you will understand why, in the end, SQL is still the go-to choice for many.

Python

Python is an open-source language created in the 1980s and made popular for its versatility, especially when using different libraries. Due to this, it is no wonder that Python has become one of the most popular languages in the present, with large companies such as Spotify, Uber, and Netflix using it for their software. "Python is a favorite for working with data because its easy integration with multiple libraries and flexibility make it easy to adapt to various formats (text, video, audio, Comma Separated Values [CSV], and web) involved with working with data" (Buuck, 2022).

One of the advantages that Python has over SQL is the fact that it presents more functionalities and possibilities for the engineer to create code and exploratory analysis. However, this does come with the disadvantage that it makes Python slower when compared to SQL, both in creating the query and in processing time. Although Python is an object-oriented language, it is just as easy to understand as SQL, despite needing to have coding experience to program efficiently. However, this process is easily managed with the thousands of different libraries available for Python, something that SQL does not have.

Challenges that are usually presented with SQL that are not found in Python are the ease of testing and debugging code. While both actions are possible to carry out in SQL, Python provides a more user-friendly manner to do this. The main reason for this is because "SQL testing libraries limit themselves to testing the data but not the code. These database testing libraries most often get executed on production as a last resort to break the data pipeline if the data is incorrect" (Pelgrim, 2022).

Finally, we must look at the scalability of each of these languages. Here, SQL has a greater advantage by having the possibility to up or downscale by adding or removing tables from the database, while this will require more effort and coding when using Python. This means that if you are dealing with a simple database that requires less or more structured queries, the way to go would be SQL since the concepts are easy to learn, and you won't have the hassle of having to execute several lines of code for one action.

Essentially speaking, Python is used for some functions and more complicated analysis, but it is unlikely to replace SQL knowledge, especially for those who are starting out with managing data. "While it may be tempting to frame the debate between SQL and Python as a stand-off, the two languages in fact excel at different parts of the data-processing pipeline" (Pelgrim, 2022).

R

Although less common than Python, R is also one of the main choices for those who are looking to explore and manage data. This language was created in the 1970s, having as its main charac-teristic a heavy mathematical background. For this reason, most of those who are looking to run statistical or data analysis choose R as their preferred language. However, similarly to Python, R presents a few disadvantages when compared to SQL, especially when considering database management.

One of the main disadvantages of R when compared to SQL is the speed of processing when dealing with large amounts of data. SQL will usually carry out the queries faster, especially when there are several rows and columns to be processed. R is also not designed to deal efficiently with database management. While it is an excellent language for statistics, data visualization, and data analysis, the coding required for handling the information for simple approaches makes it complicated because of all the coding and layers that are needed.

At the same time, R will provide the user with more alternatives for calculations and a better visualization experience. If you remember what was mentioned earlier, SQL can have quite an unfriendly interface in some cases, and in this aspect, R is significantly better. The dialects in R are also more comprehensive than those in SQL. You might require more command lines in SQL for a query when compared to R, even though it is a more user-friendly language.

According to Peck (2020), R is ideal for performing local analysis and exploring data—the tools and varied syntax enable the user to create a large range of simulations and studies. On the other hand, if what you are looking for is to transform and make the data ready to be presented, then your option should be SQL for the easy approach it presents. Finally, you should remember that SQL will have optimal performance in cloud applications and warehouses, making it easier to manage the data from anywhere.

Quick Overview

To make the differences between Python, R, and SQL even clearer, let's take a look at this comparative table with all their characteristics:

Language	SQL	Python	R
Language Application	Ideal for databases	General purposes	Statistics and data analysis
Ease of Use	User-friendly	Requires coding	Requires coding and math knowledge
Performance	Fast for database operations	Slower processing	Low performance for large datasets
Cost	Open-source	Open-source	Open-source
Functionality	Ideal for DBMS	Machine learning	Statistical analysis
Scalability	Easily scalable	May present limitations	Limited
Library Availability	Limited	Numerous libraries and packages	Large repository updated by users
Data Management	Fast management in databases	Ideal for exploration	Ideal for data manipulation
Testing	Limited features	Supports testing	Limited
Debugging	Limited features	Debugging tools available	Limited features

Now that you have learned the comprehensive basics of SQL and its advantages, it is time that we start our journey to explore more of its characteristics in depth. As we move on to the next chapter, you will learn about the SQL dialects, the different types of databases that can be used, and what operational systems they are compatible with. Read on to see what the best options for your project are and how each can be applied.

Chapter 2
SQL Dialects and Databases

As you have read before, when considering SQL, it is important to keep in mind that there is not only ANSI SQL, but also ISO SQL, and several other dialects that change according to the company or database you are using. Understanding these differences is important, so you can identify which variation of SQL you are going to need and apply to the database you will use. Remember that databases can have different sizes: from those that are small and can be stored in a computer or a file system, to large ones that will be held in a database server or the cloud.

Whether the DBMS is being used for marketing, finance, data science, or even social media, you will see that there are several options when looking for an efficient way to extract, modify, and manage data. In this chapter, you are going to learn about some of the different SQL dialects used in the market, as well as the SQL DBMS they are compatible with. Once you are done reading this chapter, you will be able to identify the best database to fulfill your project's needs—the first step into starting to build your own portfolio!

A Closer Look at SQL

To understand the concept of SQL dialects, let's suppose for a minute that you do not know how to speak English, but want to learn for several reasons. Just as any other language widely spoken, English has its differences between, for example, the United Kingdom and the United States. If you think about it, even within these, there are certain terms and slang words that are characteristic of a region.

This same analogy can be applied to SQL dialects. First, you have the ANSI/ISO standards, which would represent the "basic" English, with terms and expressions that are used independently of where you are. This is the type of English that anyone would understand since it is made of universal terms and commonly used vocabulary. However, if you go to a specific region in either location, they might still use the main English structure but add their own jargon and vocabulary to certain things. In this case, these regional dialects would be the same as the SQL dialects.

This means that the language you are using is still English (SQL), but it has variations according to the location (DBMS) where you are (you are using). To complete the analogy, we can say that if you learn English (SQL) you will be able to understand most of the people who speak the language in whichever country you go to (databases). However, it is important to understand that each of these countries will have their own variation of English (dialect) and to fully understand what they are saying, you will need to learn a new "version" of the language (databases using their own SQL version).

SQL vs. NoSQL

Now that you have a clear idea of how SQL and its dialects relate to each other (and we will get back to that in a minute), it is also important that you take a minute to refresh your memory about something that has already been mentioned. You already know that SQL is used for relational databases or RDBMS. However, it is also common to hear in the market the term NoSQL, which means "not only SQL." When this term is used, it is usually referring to nonrelational databases, or at least a DBMS that does not only have relational databases.

This language is generally used for databases that do not have a fixed structure, meaning that the data is not distributed between rows and columns. In addition to this, when referring to SQL, you have a general standard and other dialects that vary from it, and learning the basic structure will enable you to have a certain understanding of the specific dialects. On the other hand, when we are speaking about NoSQL, the dialects can greatly vary between each database that is being used, meaning that there is no specific standard or consistency among them.

Although they differ in structure, properties, scalability, query language, and support, the decision will ultimately be based on how they are going to be applied to the data gathered by a business. While SQL will be ideal for smaller and structured data, NoSQL should be used when the data is constantly changed and there is the need to carry out a deeper analysis of the data you are using. Many companies decide to use both languages, depending on the objective of the analysis.

The best option will depend on your choice, although you should remember that ultimately, SQL is a language that has been largely tested, has amazing support, and is incredibly time-efficient. Due to this, according to Talend (n.d.), "When in doubt, SQL is usually more appropriate, as RDBMSs are better supported and fault-tolerant."

Understanding SQL Dialects

Knowing that SQL has different dialects is crucial to identifying which standard should be applied to your RDBMS. Essentially speaking, your dialect choice will directly depend on the database you are going to use. Although they all stream from the same SQL ANSI/ISO standard, "it is rare to write SQL that will perfectly work across many database platforms. There will be variations that exist among different databases" (Berry, 2021). While these differences are usually small or relate only to certain keywords, knowing when to use each one will be the determining factor for efficient database management.

While "learning an entire dialect could take years to master, we should keep in mind that syntax basics are all the same" (Berry, 2021). This means that by learning the basic keywords for ANSI/ISO SQL, you will already have a significant advantage in having a better understanding of the specific dialects. Some examples that can be named that are used in the market include SQLAlchemy, DQSL, Jet SQL, and DQSL. However, the previously mentioned are not as common as the three dialects that will be discussed in more depth in this book. These are PL/SQL, T-SQL, MySQL, and PL/sgSQL, which have the following characteristics:

- **PL/SQL:** Procedural Language for SQL is the SQL dialect used by Oracle databases. It has more functionalities than the original SQL and allows for a more versatile and comprehensive management of SQL functions.

- **T-SQL:** is the short for Transact-SQL, the version of SQL for Microsoft databases and software. Here, the only exception is Access, which has a SQL dialect of its own.
- **MySQL:** The name of the dialect is the same as the database. This dialect of SQL is the most similar to ANSI/ISO SQL, with just a few modifications and differences.
- **PL/sgSQL:** Also known as Procedural Language/PostgreSQL, this dialect is used by the PostgreSQL databases. It has a similar structure and functions to PL/SQL.

Now that you are aware of the SQL dialects we will be looking deeper into in this book, it is time to see some of the main characteristics of the DBMS that use them. As you move on to the next section, you will learn about the most popular database systems currently used, their main characteristics, and their best applications. As mentioned earlier, since these are the most commonly used RDBMS, they will be the ones we will focus on in this book, although this does not mean that there aren't other available options you can choose from in the market.

SQL Databases

Recent research has shown that the top three currently most used RDBMS in the market are Oracle, MySQL, and Microsoft SQL Server (Taylor, 2023). While all of these are paid RDBMS managed by a specific corporation, there are also a few open-sourced management systems that can be used, such as MariaDB and PostgreSQL. This might make you wonder which of them is the best to use and to adopt for your company. That is a very good question—although paid databases are usually the go-to solution for many companies, looking at PostgreSQL can be an alternative to saving money for business operations.

Oracle

To start understanding the difference between each RDBMS, we are going to first look into the Oracle databases. One of the reasons for this specific DBMS to be widely used by companies is that it has an extremely high performance when compared to others. Another feature that attracts many of its users is the ability it has to carry out data backup and recovery, although this will require payment for additional storage. However, according to Singh (2019), "the best advantage that users get when they make use of the Oracle database is that it easily manages the multiple databases within the same transaction."

Other features we could mention are the large range of client support offered and innovation processes to improve its DBMS and portability capacity. "The Oracle database is ported to all different platforms than all other its competition. It easily runs on almost 20 networking protocols and also on more than 100 hardware platforms" (Singh, 2019). However, when considering implementing or creating a project in an Oracle DBMS, it is also important to think about the disadvantages it has, which should also be noted.

The two greatest points that should be mentioned are the cost and the difficulty of operating the system. Because it is backed by a company, there is the need to pay for licenses, operating fees, storage costs, and additional services. According to Sullivan (2015), this cost can be as much as 10 times higher when compared to other competitors, without considering how much you will need to pay for a specialized administrator to run the database. Because of the difficulty of learning PL/SQL, professionals who can efficiently operate the DBMS can be costly to the employer when compared to other professionals.

Since PL/SQL was mentioned, let's take a closer look into the challenges and possibilities this dialect offers the user and what are the main elements you should keep in mind. Although this is not intended to be an exhaustive list of features, syntax, and details that characterize the dialect, you will be given some of the main aspects of PL/SQL, as well as the most important advantages, differences, and features that make it up. In case you are interested in learning more, it is possible to look up the official documentation on the Oracle website.

Some of the main features of PL/SQL include the possibility to use different data types and check errors, the support for object-oriented programming, and the ability to apply different programming structures to it (Tutorials Point, n.d.-a). The language is highly portable and allows addressing the database with large blocks of code at once. It is also a secure and productive language, enhanced by its portable characteristics and design variation possibilities.

To start using PL/SQL, you will need to download a tool that is called the PL/SQL developer. If you are going to install the program, you should be aware that there are certain requirements your computer should have. According to Component Source (n.d.), the software is compatible with "Windows XP, 2003, 2008, Vista, Windows 7, Windows 8, Windows 10 and Windows 11. The supported Oracle Server versions are 7.x, 8.x, 8i, 9i, 10g, 11g, 12c, 18c, 19c, 21c, and 23c on any platform."

Speaking specifically about the language, there are three main elements you should know:

1. All the codes will start with the keyword "DECLARE," which is *optional*. In this case, you are going to state the classes, variables, subprograms, and any other elements you are going to use in the code.
2. Next, you will have the code in itself and the commands you want it to execute. It will be written between the keywords "BEGIN" and "END."
3. If there are any exceptions or errors you want the program to handle, you will then use the last keyword, "EXCEPTION," which is also optional for the code you are creating. In case you decide to use this keyword, it should be applied between the BEGIN and END keywords so that it can be recognized as part of the code's execution.

For all the above instances, it is important to remember that all the statements you declare need to be finalized with a semicolon to be recognized by the program. In PL/SQL, the semicolon is a delimiter, which means that it is a character with a specific function within the program. Each language will have its own delimiters, and it is important to study them and memorize as best as possible what they are to ensure your code has no errors. Two of the other delimiters that are worth mentioning are the double dash (--) used to add comments to the code that occupy one line, and the /* and */, which are used to begin and end comments in the code that have more than one line.

The last thing you should know when referring to PL/SQL is that there are four types of data that are accepted by the code. They are numbers (that are used to perform operations), alphanumeric characters, date and time, and Boolean statements for logic operations. While there are other subtypes after these that are also important, getting into detail for each of these is rather extensive and, therefore, will not be described in detail in this book.

You should also know that in PL/SQL (as well as in other dialects) you will need to understand concepts such as variables, constants, and literals. It is also important to be familiar with the mathematical operators that can be used, as well as how to apply procedures, packages, and cursors. These will all be different according to the dialect you use, and it is no different in PL/SQL.

A comprehensive guide with all the relevant information is available on the Oracle.com website, which contains the official documentation for PL/SQL in different languages. On the website, you will find resources that explain the different structures, collections, packages, triggers, and more. If this dialect is the one that interests you, I encourage you to access the free content available and learn about its specificities and details to enhance your programming experience.

MySQL

As the name of this RDBMS suggests, MySQL is a relational database created to be used with SQL as its main query language, although today it is possible to use with other languages such as C+, PHP, and Java. One of the main reasons many users are attracted to this system is because it is open source, meaning there is no cost to implement it despite having its rights owned by Oracle. If the user wants to use this RDBMS, all they have to do is access MySQL.com and download the program on their computer for no cost.

Another feature that makes it attractive is its increased speed when compared to other RDBMS, even when dealing with larger amounts of data. This makes it an ideal solution for using larger data sets with millions of rows. In addition to this, since this RDBMS was created for the specific purpose of warehousing and managing large data sets, you will be able to easily upscale its capacity if needed. It is also important to consider that because it is open-source software, you will have two great advantages: a large community for online support and troubleshooting and the increased availability of repositories with code you can reuse.

Its flexibility to be used on several operational systems (OS), such as Windows, macOS, Ubuntu, and Linux, makes it versatile and adaptable to the current setup you have available. This portable feature makes it an attractive option for businesses, along with an architecture characteristic that enables programs to connect to the database and manage the information. Lastly, you should know that MySQL is considered the most secure and reliable DBMS in the market, used by large companies such as Facebook, X (formerly Twitter), and WordPress (Techstrikers, 2019).

You should also know that MySQL has a simple system that is easy to understand. In addition to this, the SQL dialect that can be used in this database is the one that most resembles the ANSI/ISO SQL, with minor changes and adjustments, making the learning process easier and simpler for the first-time user. "MySQL makes many concessions to supporting the widest possible variety of data structures, from the standard but rich logical, numeric, alphanumeric, date, and time types, to more advanced JSON or geospatial data" (Talend, 2023).

However, regardless of all the attractive features that MySQL has, there are also a few disadvantages that should be considered if this is going to be your choice of RDBMS. The first is that most of the information you will need to rely on is going to be based in communities, since the debugging and development of the database is not as efficient when compared to others that are paid and have prompt support. In addition to this, if there are any constraints with SQL, checks are not supported, leading to errors in the code you are developing.

It is also considered a limited software, susceptible to handling certain transactions, which may lead to corruption of the data being used. There is also the need for node maintenance manually, since there is no support for auto sharding, making it challenging for some scaling procedures (Mayankanand2701, 2022). Finally, you should be aware that there might be some restrictions for versions previous to the 5.0 (the current version is the 8.0), and that you might need to pay for additional features such as memory increase, support services, larger backup capabilities, and out-of-scope analytic tools.

Microsoft SQL Server

The Microsoft SQL Server, also known as MS SQL Server, is also an RDBMS that was developed by the company for database management and continues to be one of the pieces of software available in their product portfolio. Much like the previous two RDBMSs that you have seen, it is mainly operated with a SQL dialect, although this is a specific one for this RDBMS known as T-SQL. MS SQL Server is a paid database, with the price starting at approximately $14,000 per license for the premium version.

One of the main advantages of this RDBMS is that it has different editions, each designed for a specific purpose. On the Microsoft website, you will find from the express version, which is free and is suitable for learning processes and for small data-driven applications, to the enterprise version, which is the premium service offered by the company and has remarkable characteristics such as speed, enhanced performance, business intelligence tools, and another wide range of services that are perfect for companies who critically use data.

Another positive point of MS SQL Server is the possibility of using the express version to learn and test the tool for free while having access to all its enterprise features. In addition to this, if you consider that MS SQL Server can be integrated with other Microsoft applications, this makes its attractiveness increase, especially if you consider its collaboration, visualization, data model, and information management tools. Among those that can be used in association with it are Power BI and Azure Data Studio, both of which enable the development of dashboards and reports with the data it contains.

Microsoft also provides comprehensive documentation for the MS SQL Server features online and free of charge. This means that apart from the customer service it offers, it enables the database manager to troubleshoot online on the website for its different versions and uses. Lastly, you should know that this RDBMS not only runs in Windows versions, but it is also supported by some versions of Linux starting in SQL Server versions after 2017. Nevertheless, even if you are going to run it on Windows, it is important to check the version you are going to use, since there might be compatibility limitations.

When speaking about documentation, the same availability is true when referring to T-SQL. On the official Microsoft page, it is possible to find a reference guide for the dialect that includes the supported data types, how to manage date and time, the functions accepted, the best alternatives to carry out queries, and how to create statements, among other resources. While the syntax has its differences when compared to other dialects, it will bring similar results when the queries are carried out (Microsoft Learn, 2023). One example is a feature that enables all commands to be submitted to the server at once, instead of using individual queries as used by other dialects.

One of the unique features that T-SQL offers the developer is the ability to carry out data and string processing with several support functions. These include six main functions and several additional sub-functions or categories, which provide versatility to the user regardless if they are working with a collection or one single value. When combined in the statements with the relevant keywords, operators, variables, and other dialect elements, the developer will find it enables countless opportunities to manage and work with the database.

PostgreSQL

The last RDBMS that will be mentioned is PostgreSQL. This RDBMS, which was previously known as Postgres, is free and open source and supports both relational and nonrelational queries. It is usually applied for several industries, especially those that have websites dealing with a large amount of data or need to analyze and create dynamic interactions and extract complex analysis from the data set. It is also for these reasons that it is widely applied in the scientific industries that deal with research and need to carry out complex queries with the available data (Peterson, 2023a).

While being free is definitely an advantage for such a powerful RDBMS, there are other reasons why developers and companies select this database for use. First is the compatibility with different OS including Windows, Linux, Unix, macOS, and Solaris. This is a positive point from the portability aspect and the versatility to be applied to different organizations. The next advantage is the ability to use different programming languages with tools such as Java, Go, Ruby, Python, and C+ and the large online community that has been working with it for the past 20 years, since its development.

PostgreSQL is also considered to have all the ACID properties required from an RDBMS, making it highly reliable. It should also be mentioned that it provides the developer with the possibility to use and support geographic objects and information, enabling the processing of complex geospatial data to create location-based services. Lastly, despite its robust structure and complex processing abilities, PostgreSQL is easy to use, understand, and learn. This makes it the perfect alternative for some companies who are willing to structure their data with low costs and maintenance while still ensuring quality.

On the other hand, PostgreSQL has some disadvantages when compared to the other popular databases in the market. One of them is that since there is no company backing up the program, it is difficult to "market" its usability and find support for certain open-source apps that work with other types of RDBMS. Being free and not owned by a specific company also means that there is no specific client service for troubleshooting and client support, although the community has several online groups with experienced developers and documentation.

It should also be mentioned that PostgreSQL has its own dialect of SQL, as mentioned earlier. Known as PL/pgSQL, this dialect is very similar to the one used by Oracle and comes embedded with the RDBMS once it is installed. Since it is a native dialect, it means that it is trusted by the PostgreSQL database server, making it one of the most accessible options for those looking to start using the database even without prior knowledge of coding. As with most of the SQL dialects, it is an easy-to-learn option with comprehensive online documentation that can be accessed on the PostgreSQL.org website.

Quick Overview

After reading about the main RDBMS used in the market, here is a quick reference table that will help you compare and analyze their characteristics.

RDBMS	Oracle	MySQL	MS SQL Server	PostgreSQL
Native Dialect	PL/SQL	MySQL	T-SQL	PL/pgSQL
Cost	Commercial	Open-source and commercial	Commercial	Open-source
OS	AIX, HP-UX, Linux, OS X, Solaris, Windows, z/OS	FreeBSD, Linux, OS X, Solaris, and Windows	Windows and Linux	FreeBSD, HP-UX, Linux, NetBSD, OpenBSD, OS X, Solaris, Unix, and Windows
Data Types	Structured, semi-structured, and unstructured	Semi-structured and structured	Structured, semi-structured, and unstructured	Structured, semi-structured, and unstructured

The Bottom Line

You now have a complete overview of the main RDBMS and the SQL dialects that can be used with them. While the previous description of these is not comprehensive, it gives you the main highlights that will help you better understand the applications, advantages, and disadvantages they each have. As you might have noticed, there is no right or wrong option to choose from. This decision will exclusively depend on your needs, budget, OS, and preference according to the project you are working on and the objective you are trying to achieve.

It is also understandable if you are unable to make this decision right now. There is still so much more to learn and to understand before you can choose which path to take. For this reason, as we move on to the next chapter, you are going to learn about the SQL basics, which are the data types and structures, something I like to call SQL 101. As you read, it will be possible to take a closer look into the characteristics of each mentioned dialect and their applications. While this will likely not be the determining factor that will guide your selection, it will certainly help you obtain some insight into the differences, challenges, and possibilities each of them can provide for your future project.

Chapter 3
Sql 101

Understanding the basics of SQL and the differences between each of the main dialects will be the starting point of your learning journey. This will be the foundation that will allow you to carry out queries and build statements and structures that will be used to manage the database. For this reason, you will learn all about data types, data structures, and tables.

Think about it as driving different types of vehicles. Theoretically speaking, driving a car, a bus, or a truck is essentially the same. They will all have the gear, the acceleration pedal, and the brakes. However, each of them will require a specific type of knowledge that is unique to the transportation method you are driving. When driving each of these transportation means, you will have to consider the differences between automatic and manual shifting, the size of the vehicle, and the speed limitations.

The same can be applied to the SQL dialects. While we have the general standard of SQL, ANSI/ISO SQL, which would be the common point for all the SQL languages, each of these dialects will have its own particularities and specificities that should be taken into consideration. This means there will be variations between the syntax, data types, and keywords each of them uses. They will all come from the "universal" standard, but each of them will have their own adaptation of how to be used.

For this reason, in this chapter, you will be taught not only the general ANSI/ISO standard, but also the different variations that can be found within the four main SQL dialects: PL/SQL, MySQL, T-SQL, and PL/pgSQL. As you will see, despite having their differences, they all have "SQL" as part of their name.

SQL Syntax

All programming languages have a specific structure, or syntax, which sets the standard and the guidelines on how they should be used. In ANSI/ISO SQL, when you ask the program to perform a command, you must create a statement (or command) that will tell it what you want it to do. These statements usually begin with keywords such as "delete," "select," "update," and others.

One of the essential characteristics you should know about SQL is that, differently from other programming languages, it is not case-sensitive, which means that writing "DELETE" will be the same as "delete." This is an important piece of information to have, since some dialects will have this distinction and it may affect the query you are going to carry out. In addition to this, you should also know that after these commands, you will need to add a semicolon (;) so the action can be recognized.

If you wanted to use a specific database (in this case, named "my_database"), for example, you would use:

```
USE my_database;
```

Or if you wanted to insert data in a specific table (in this case, named "fruit"), you would use the code:

```
INSERT INTO FRUIT (ID,TYPE,PRICE) VALUES
(1, 'apple', 5.00),
(2, 'pear', 3.00),
(3, 'orange', 4.00);
```

In the above example, it is possible to identify that we are giving the command (making the statement) in upper case letters with the command "INSERT" and that we are telling the database to insert into the "FRUIT" table three elements into empty rows with the names "apple," "pear," and "orange," each with their own price. You will also notice that after the last element, there is the semicolon, which means that this is the end of the statement. If you wanted to add more elements to the list, then all you would need to do is to continue adding the ID number, the fruit, and the price, and finalize it with a semicolon.

Each of the statements in SQL will have its own characteristics and particularities depending on the keyword you are going to use. For a quick reference guide on the statement structure, including the keyword that would be used and the syntax that should be applied, here is a table you can use with the most common elements:

Keyword	Function	Syntax
ALTER DATABASE	Changes a database structure.	ALTER DATABASE db_name {action you want to carry out};
ALTER TABLE	Changes the structure of a table.	ALTER TABLE table_name {select action} column_name {data_type};
CREATE DATABASE	Creates a new database.	CREATE DATABASE db_name;
CREATE INDEX	Creates an index on a table belonging to the database.	CREATE UNIQUE INDEX index_name ON table_name (column1, column2,...);
CREATE TABLE	Creates a new table. *Note: To create the new table, you will need to open parentheses at the end of the command before inputting data.*	CREATE TABLE table_name (column_1 data, column_2 data, ... PRIMARY KEY (reference column));
DELETE FROM	Deletes a part of the table without having to delete it entirely.	DELETE FROM table_name WHERE {INSERT CONDITION};
DROP DATABASE	Deletes a database.	DROP DATABASE db_name;
DROP INDEX	Deletes an index from a table.	DROP INDEX index_name ON table_name;
DROP TABLE	Deletes an entire table from a database.	DROP TABLE table_name;
INSERT INTO	Inserts data in the table. *Note that in the "columns," you are going to name each of the columns in the table and then in the values place the information of what you want to add.*	INSERT INTO table_name (column_1, column_2...) VALUES (value1, value2...);
SELECT	Chooses data from a certain table based on the columns available.	SELECT column_1, column_2 FROM table_name;

UPDATE	Updates information on a table, similar to an "if" statement. You will establish the location of the element you want to modify and what you want to modify it with.	UPDATE table_name SET column1 = value1, column2 = value2 = new_value [WHERE];
USE	Indicates the database or table you will use.	USE db_name; USE table_name;

These are some of the most common keywords and syntaxes used in SQL, although several others can also be used for distinct purposes. Learning these and knowing how to apply them is a great place to start and will significantly impact your journey in learning how to manage these RDBMS. However, it is not all about the syntax: The administrator must also learn what are the types of data that can be used in these databases.

As we move along to the next section of this chapter, you are going to learn about the different SQL data types and how they differ in each of the dialects we have talked about. You will see that there are different ways to store the information in the database such as numbers, alphanumeric characters, and even the specific application of date and time. It is by using these data types that you will determine the characteristics of each column and store the necessary values accordingly.

SQL Data Types

A data type is the format in which the values will be stored in the database. Since these RDBMS can be used in the most diverse industries, this means that they should also be able to use different "formats" of the information. For example, a supermarket might need to store letters and prices, while a factory might need to register the time and date an employee enters and leaves the premises. To make these distinct applications possible and to enable SQL to interact with them, you will need to define what is expected in each of the cells in the columns.

Most specialists divide these data types into three categories, each with their own subcategories. They are string, numeric, and date and time data types. There are also some data types that do not fit into any of these previous categories, so we are going to call them "miscellaneous data types."

String Data Types

The first data types we are going to look into are what are known as string data types. These will usually accept alphanumeric characters and will be used to store information that is not specifically related to numbers.

Character String

The data types belonging to this subcategory have a maximum length accepted for the number of characters (although they can be fixed or variable).

Data Type	Description
CHARACTER	A character string with a fixed length. Values are usually alphanumeric and should be placed inside quotation marks.
CHARACTER VARYING (VARCHAR)	A character string with variable length and fixed maximum length.
CHARACTER LARGE OBJECT (CLOB)	Used for a collection of character data in an RDBMS. These are usually stored in a separate location but referenced within the table.
NATIONAL CHARACTER	Is the same as the CHARACTER data type but supports multibyte or Unicode characters.
NATIONAL CHARACTER VARYING	Is the same as the CHARACTER VARYING data type but supports multibyte or Unicode characters.
NATIONAL CHARACTER LARGE OBJECT	Is the same as the CHARACTER LARGE OBJECT (CLOB) data type but supports multibyte or Unicode characters.

Binary String

The binary string types are used to store binary data in the database and can be fixed or varied lengths. They are divided into the following:

Data Type	Description
BINARY	Used to store binary units with a fixed length, which are usually 0 or 1.
BINARY VARYING	Used to store binary strings with a maximum but variable length.
BINARY LARGE OBJECT (BLOB)	Used to store long sequences of bytes.

Boolean

These are used to store values that use logic by defining the column name as BOOLEAN, in which the possible answers can only be TRUE or FALSE.

Numeric Data Types

As the name suggests, these data types are those that are composed of numbers. These are composed of five formats for exact numbers and four for approximate numbers. They are the following:

Data Type	Description
INTEGER	Used to store a numerical integer (no decimal). The maximum length of 10 characters and variable size within the threshold to be defined by the user (p).
SMALLINT	Used to store a numerical integer (no decimal) with a maximum length of 5 characters.
BIGINT	Used to store a numerical integer (no decimal) with a maximum length of 19 characters.
NUMERIC	Exact number with a decimal point. The standard used is to define precision "p" and scale "s". *Example*: NUMERIC(6,3) is a number that has 3 digits before the decimal and 3 digits after the decimal.
DECIMAL	Exact number with a decimal point. Same as NUMERIC.
REAL	Approximate numerical expression with a precision of 7.
DOUBLE PRECISION	Approximate numerical expression with a precision of 16.
FLOAT	Approximate numerical expression with a precision of 16.
DECFLOAT	Approximate numerical expression with a precision of 34.

Date and Time Data Types

The last of the structured data types are those belonging to the date and time. These will be used to store this specific information, most of the time formatting according to the standard established by the database. Here are the five variations that can be used to store these data types:

Data Type	Description
DATE	Stores year, month, and day values in the YYYY-MM-DD format.
TIME WITHOUT TIMEZONE	Stores hours, minutes, and seconds values in HH:MM:SS format, *without* considering the time zone the database is
TIMESTAMP WITHOUT TIMEZONE	Stores year, month, day, hours, minutes, and seconds values in YYYY-MM-DD HH:MM:SS format *without* considering the time zone the database is located in.
TIME WITH TIMEZONE	Stores hours, minutes, and seconds values in HH:MM:SS format, considering the time zone the database is located in.
TIMESTAMP WITH TIMEZONE	Stores year, month, day, hours, minutes, and seconds values in YYYY-MM-DD HH:MM:SS format, considering the time zone the database is located in.

Miscellaneous Data Types

Lastly, we have the miscellaneous, or other data types, which are those that do not fit into any of the previous categories. These include, but are not limited to, the following:

- **Array data types:** Used to store array values.
- **Interval data types:** Used to specify a range of dates or times within the database by using INTERVAL DAY and INTERVAL YEAR.
- **JSON data types:** Used for storing data in JSON format in the database.
- **Multiset:** Used to store an unordered collection of elements with variable length.
- **XML data types:** Used to store data in XML format in the database.

While in this section you have been presented with the different data types available in SQL, it is important to remember that this ANSI/SQL vocabulary may not apply to all the databases available in the market since each RDBMS will have its own interpretation and application. For this reason, in the following sections, you are going to learn about the difference in vocabulary when using each dialect for the databases we have seen before.

However, in order to avoid information that you already have, the focus of these will be on the data types that are different or that can be converted. This means that you will be reading about the data types that are *different* between the ANSI/ISO SQL standard and the dialect for each database. At the end of the chapter, a table will be provided with the comparison between all four dialects to enhance the learning process and comprehension of the differences among them.

Oracle Data Types

When we refer to Oracle databases, we are speaking about those that use the PL/SQL dialect. This means that it is composed of data types native to the RDBMS and those that can be converted. In this section, you are going to learn about these built-in datatypes, those that can be supplied by Oracle, and finally, the data types that are comparable to ANSI/ISO SQL. It is important to know that despite having its own language, Oracle uses precompilers to recognize other data types that come from other dialects also commonly used in RDBMS, known as external data types by the organization (Oracle Help Center, n.d.).

According to Oracle's official documentation, the data types used in their databases can be divided with the following structure:

- **Oracle built-in data types**

  - character data types
  - number data types
  - long and raw data types
  - datetime data types
  - large object data types
  - ROWID data types

- **ANSI-supported data types**
- **User-defined data types**
- **Oracle-supplied data types**

  - any data types
  - XML data types
  - spatial data types

Just as you have seen in the previous section, you will be provided with tables that contain the main data types in Oracle PL/SQL and a final explanation of which ANSI/ISO SQL data types are converted when using the dialect. Although the list will not be exhaustive, you will find it to be comprehensive with the main data types that can be used with these RDBMS. In this section, the user-defined data types will not be approached, since their application will vary according to each user. All the information in this section was extracted from the official Oracle documentation in Oracle Help Center (n.d.).

Oracle Built-in Data Types

In this first section of the Oracle PL/SQL data types, we are going to look into those that are built-in for Oracle, which means they belong to the native dialect and might not work for other databases apart from those in Oracle. It is important to remark that while some of them might have the same name as those in the ANSI/ISO SQL standard, they might have a different functionality or length from these. Below, you will find the different subcategories for each of these data types.

Character Data Types

Data Type	Description	Syntax
CHAR	Used for alphanumeric characters in string format. Is used to store information that is both in characters or bytes (1 to 2,000).	CHAR (size CHAR) CHAR (size BYTE) (Byte is usually set as the standard if none is defined.)
NCHAR	Used for storage of a Unicode character value with a fixed length that can range from 1 to 2,000 bytes.	NCHAR (size)
NVARCHAR2	Used for storage of variable length Unicode character values that can range from 1 to 4,000 bytes.	NVARCHAR2 (size) 32,767 bytes is the upper limit if you are using MAX_STRING_SIZE = EXTENDED and 4,000 bytes is the upper limit if you are using MAX_STRING_SIZE = STANDARD
VARCHAR2	Used for storage of variable length alphanumeric character values that can range from 1 to 4,000 bytes. Uses the same syntax as the CHAR data type.	CHAR (size CHAR) CHAR (size BYTE) 32,767 bytes is the upper limit if you are using MAX_STRING_SIZE = EXTENDED and 4,000 bytes is the upper limit if you are using MAX_STRING_SIZE = STANDARD

Number Data Types

When you want to express numbers in an Oracle database, it might be required that you insert into the syntax of the number the precision (the number of integral digits that can range from 1 to 38), or "p," and the scale (the number of decimal points the number can have), or "s." Here are the numeric data types you should consider for PL/SQL:

Data Type	Description	Syntax
NUMBER	Used to express a whole or decimal number that will be expressed in the table.	NUMBER (p,s)
FLOAT	Used to express a floating number in which the precision can range from 1 to 126 binary digits.	FLOAT (p) (The values required are from 1 to 22 bytes.)
BINARY_FLOAT	Used to express a 32-bit floating point number.	BINARY_FLOAT (The data type requires 4 bytes.)
BINARY_DOUBLE	Used to express a 64-bit floating point number.	BINARY_DOUBLE (The data type requires 8 bytes.)

Long and Raw Data Types

These data types are used to store binary data in the database. They have a size limit of storage size and are commonly used to store audio files, images, and other large objects in the database. Here are the three data types that can be used for this purpose.

Data Type	Description	Syntax
LONG	Used to store characters of data that have a maximum length of 2 GB or 2^{31} -1 bytes.	LONG Available to provide the user with backward compatibility with other data types.
RAW	Used to store raw binary data in bytes in the database table. A size should be specified when you are using this data type. Data in this category can be indexed.	RAW (size) Maximum size is 32,767 bytes if you are using MAX_STRING_SIZE = EXTENDED and Maximum size is 2,000 bytes if you are using MAX_STRING_SIZE = STANDARD
LONG RAW	Used to store raw binary data in bytes with variable length. Data in this category cannot be indexed.	LONG RAW Maximum storage value is 2 GB.

Date and Time Data Types

The date and time data types in PL/SQL have the same purpose as those in ANSI/ISO SQL, although they have a different range when compared to the latter and a different exhibition structure. Here are the time and date data types that can be used with Oracle:

Data Type	Description	Syntax
DATE	Establishes the range according to the date that is logged into the database, ranging from January 1, 4712 BC to December 31, 9999 AD. Fixed size of 7 bytes.	DATE CURRENT_DATE Displayed as standard in the DD-MMM-YY HH-MM-SS format. Does not apply the time zone of where the database is located.
TIMESTAMP	Establishes the year, month, day, hours, minutes, and seconds in the database. Can be used to determine fractions of seconds from 0–9 with 6 as a standard. Variable size of 7 or 11 bytes for standard time. A fixed size of 13 bytes for the timestamp with time zone.	TIMESTAMP (fractional_seconds_precision) The default format parameter: NLS_TIMESTAMP_FORMAT parameter. TIMESTAMP (fractional_seconds_precision) WITH TIME ZONE The default format parameter: NLS_TIMESTAMP_TZ_FORMAT parameter. Exhibited according to the time zone to which the database is set.
INTERVAL YEAR	Stores a period in years and months. Necessary to establish the year_precision for how many digits the year should exhibit.	INTERVAL YEAR [(year_precision)] TO MONTH Fixed size of 5 bytes and values from 0–9.
INTERVAL DAY	Stores a period in days, hours, minutes, and seconds. Need to establish day_precision for the maximum number of digits in the DAY datetime field. Need to establish the fractional_seconds_precision for the number of digits in the fractional part of the SECOND field.	INTERVAL DAY [(day_precision)] TO SECOND [(fractional_seconds_precision)] Fixed size of 11 bytes. Accepted values from 0–9.

Large Object (LOB) Data Types

These data types are used to store large objects within the database or in a place external to it. Is applicable for alphanumeric characters, Unicode characters, or binary objects. Here are the data types that should be used for objects with each of these characteristics:

Data Type	Description
BLOB	Used for large binary objects with a maximum size of (4 GB -1) * (database block size). Stores the information internally in the database.
CLOB	Used for large objects with single or multibyte alphanumeric characters. Can be applied to fixed or variable length. The maximum size is calculated by using: Used for large binary objects with a maximum size of (4 GB -1) * (database block size). Is used to store data internally in the database.
NCLOB	Used for large objects Unicode characters. Can be applied to fixed or variable length. The maximum size is calculated by using: Used for large binary objects with a maximum size of (4 GB -1) * (database block size). Is used to store data internally in the database.
BFILE	Used to store large objects in an external location from the database. Applies to unstructured data that has a read-only characteristic. Maximum size of 4 GB.

ROWID Data Types

When you use the ROWID data types, the request that is being made is to identify the logical or unique address of the data in the database rows. In this case, the column will be named according to the data type you want it to return, which can be one of two:

Data Type	Description	Syntax
ROWID	Base 64 string that shows the unique address of the data in a table row.	Set the column standard to ROWID.
UROWID	Base 64 string that shows the logical address of the data in a table row that is organized by indexes.	UROWID (size) The size is optional and can be declared to limit the size of the column. The default and maximum size is 4,000 bytes.

As you have seen in this section, although there are some data types that have the same name in the PL/SQL dialect as in the

ANSI/ISO standard, they have some differences in syntax, size, or application. These built-in data types provide additional features than when only applying ANSI/ISO SQL. However, there are also Oracle-supplied types that can be used as interfaces when those in ANSI/ISO are not enough. As you will see in the next section, they are composed of three subcategories and several different data types.

Oracle-Supplied Data Types

Oracle-supplied data types are those that can be implemented in other languages, and the structure to make the data work in the database will be provided by the company. When considering these interfaces, one of the most common applications is to create objects defined by the user, although they "are also used by Oracle to create some commonly useful data types. Several such data types are supplied with the server, and they serve both broad horizontal application areas (for example, the Any types) and specific vertical ones" (Oracle Help Centers, n.d.).

These data types are divided into three categories:

- **Any types:** Used to model parameters and columns when the tables do not have a known type. Adds versatility to the RDBMS and can also be used to convert other SQL dialects to work in the database. The four data types of this category are ANYTYPE, ANYDATA, and ANYDATASET.
- **Spatial types:** These data types will be used to store related to geometric figures and spatial objects that are required to be in the database. It is usually used in association with another Oracle program named Graph and will enable the user to develop applications that access locations and a geographic information system.

- **XML types:** Similar to the XML data type in ANSI/ISO SQL, this type of modeling is used to store and query data contained in XML formats in a database. It can also be used to adapt the XML data in the file to the tables you are going to use in the database.

  ○ **URL data types:** Used for the specific application of adding XML files that are in the format of a URL. These can have or not have a direct link to the external web page or file which is accessed by the database by using a HTTP address.

ANSI/ISO and PL/SQL Data Type Conversion

When comparing the different data types between Oracle PL/SQL and ANSI/ISO SQL, there are a few that are accepted but converted when inserted into the database table. This is the case for the data types we will see below, which are supplied in Oracle Help Center (n.d.).

ANSI SQL Data Type	Oracle Data Type
• CHARACTER • CHAR	CHAR
• CHARACTER VARYING • CHAR VARYING	VARCHAR2
• NATIONAL CHARACTER • NATIONAL CHAR • NCHAR	NCHAR
• NATIONAL CHARACTER VARYING • NATIONAL CHAR VARYING • NCHAR VARYING	NVARCHAR2
• NUMERIC • DECIMAL	NUMBER
• INTEGER • INT • SMALLINT	NUMBER
• FLOAT • DOUBLE PRECISION • REAL	FLOAT

As you have seen, there are some similarities between the Oracle PL/SQL data types and those that can be found in ANSI/ISO SQL. However, it is likely you have also noticed that there are several different expansion features that give the user more flexibility and managing capabilities to administer the database. But this is not the only dialect that has significant differences and enhancements when compared to the standard. Next, we will move on to learn more about the MySQL data types and dialects, which you will see have more similarities than differences when compared to ANSI/ISO SQL.

MySQL Data Types

When we talk about the MySQL dialect, the main thing you should keep in mind is that this is the dialect with the most similarities when compared to ANSI/ISO SQL. This means that many of the data types are the same and have the same name as the one found in the standard. In this section, you are going to learn about the data types in MySQL, which can be divided into the following categories:

- numeric data types
- date and time data types
- string data types
- spatial data types
- JSON data types

All the information you will see in this section was extracted from the MySQL official documentation available on the website, more specifically in the MySQL 8.0 Reference Manual in MySQL (n.d.) and the links associated with it. Without further delay, let's look into the data types in MySQL that are *different* from ANSI/ISO SQL while briefly mentioning those that are the same.

Numeric Data Types

According to MySQL (n.d.), all the ANSI/SQL data types are supported by MySQL. This means that there is no difference in syntax and use for the following data types: BOOLEAN (BOOL), SMALLINT, NUMERIC, FLOAT, REAL, DOUBLE PRECISION (DOUBLE), INTEGER (INT), and DECIMAL (DEC or FIXED). In addition to this, "MySQL also treats REAL as a synonym for DOUBLE PRECISION (a nonstandard variation), unless the REAL_AS_FLOAT SQL mode is enabled" (MySQL, n.d.).

Nevertheless, there are a few numeric data types that have a few differences in syntax or application. Here is a table with the data types that are *additional* in MySQL and their definitions:

Data Type	Description
TINYINT	Refers to very small integers with a signed range of -128 to 137 and an unsigned range from 0 to 255.
MEDIUMINT	Refers to medium integers with a signed range of -8,388,608 to 8,388,607 and an unsigned range from 0 to 16,777,215.

In the above cases, there are a few details that should be noted. The first is that when using any of these data types, the keyword will be followed by the size allowed in the column, which means the maximum length of the number that can be displayed, which is 255 for all of the above-mentioned. The other is that you might have noticed that there are two different types of ranges, one for signed and one for unsigned.

When you have an *unsigned* integer (adding the word after the data type keyword), this means that the number in the column will not accept negative numbers. This means that the range applicable to the field will be reduced from the negative to the maximum number to 0 and the maximum number. There is, however, no need to declare that the file should be signed, as this is the default in the database. Finally, please note that if you add the ZEROFILL keyword to describe a column, it will immediately attribute the UNSIGNED characteristic to it.

Date and Time Data Types

MySQL has five data types available for time and date, of which some have minor differences from ANSI/ISO SQL:

- **DATE:** adopts the format YYYY-MM-DD and ranges from 1000-01-01 to 9999-12-31.
- **TIME:** used to register a time in the format HH:MM:SS with a supported range from -838:59:59 to 838:59:59.

- **DATETIME:** applies the format YYYY-MM-DD HH:MM:SS with a range from 1000-01-01 00:00:00 to 9999-12-31 23:59:59. An extra feature provided by this datatype is the possibility to add ON UPDATE or DEFAULT to the column definition so that the information is updated to the current time and date.
- **TIMESTAMP:** uses the format YYYY-MM-DD HH:MM:SS with a range from 1970-01-01 00:00:01 UTC to 2038-01-09 03:14:07 UTC. To set the column for the present date and time, it is possible to add the DEFAULT CURRENT_TIMESTAMP or ON UPDATE CURRENT_TIMESTAMP words in the column definition.
- **YEAR:** will transform the data into a four-digit year format that can range from 1901 to 2155. Although it is permitted in older versions of MySQL, two-digit years are not available in MySQL 8.0.

If you are wondering about the changes in time zones and how this can be applied in the database, MySQL (n.d.) states that TIMESTAMP is usually converted by MySQL "from the current time zone to UTC for storage, and back from UTC to the current time zone for retrieval. By default, the current time zone for each connection is the server's time. The time zone can be set on a per-connection basis." This logic does not apply to other structures, such as the DATETIME data type.

String Data Types

Although most of the data types in MySQL for string structures are the same for CHAR, VARCHAR, BINARY, BINARY VARYING (VARBINARY), and BLOB, there are a few variations of these that should be considered when using the RDBMS. They are the following:

Data Type	Description
TINYBLOB	Used for BLOBs and have a maximum length of 255 bytes.
MEDIUMBLOB	Used for BLOBs and has a maximum length of 16,777,215 bytes.
LONGBLOB	Used for BLOBs and has a maximum length of 4,294,967,295 bytes.
TINYTEXT	Strings with a maximum of 255 characters.
MEDIUMTEXT	Used for strings with a maximum length of 16,777,215 characters.
LONGTEXT	Used for strings with a maximum length of 4,294,967,295 characters.
ENUM	Is used when you want to limit the values that can be used in a column to a specific list. Has a maximum limit of 65,535 possible values that can be entered.
SET	Is used when you want to establish that the values to be used in a column can range from 0 to more within a preestablished list. Has a maximum of 64 possible values.

Please note that when you are using MySQL there is no specific keyword when you want to apply the Unicode characters in the database, just as it happens in the ANSI/ISO SQL standard. On the other hand, when considering the miscellaneous data types, MySQL will support only spatial and JSON data types in common with ANSI/ISO SQL. While it has expansion packs that can be used to enhance the use of data with these characteristics, they have the same basic characteristics as those that can be found in the standard SQL dialect.

MS SQL Server Data Types

MS SQL Server has its own SQL dialect known as T-SQL, which can be used for all Microsoft applications except Access. Just as we have seen before with other dialects, T-SQL also has data types divided into numeric, string, date and time, and miscellaneous categories. While once again there are the same data types as you have already seen in ANSI/ISO SQL, there are also some keywords that have the same spelling but different meanings or applications.

For this section in T-SQL, the same logic applied to the previous dialects will be used. When speaking about the data types that are similar to ANSI/ISO SQL, they will be briefly mentioned and named. However, when referring to those that are different in some capability, they will be explained. Finally, at the end of the section, you will be provided with a table with the equivalent ANSI/ISO SQL data types with those of T-SQL.

Once again, it is important to mention that all the information in this section was obtained from the official documentation on the Microsoft Learn (2023) website in the "Transact-SQL" section and related links.

String Data Types

In T-SQL, the string data types have three different subcategories: character string, Unicode character string, and binary. Read on to discover the main characteristics of each.

Character String

The data types belonging to this category have a maximum length that can be fixed or variable and do not accept Unicode characters.

Data Type	Description
CHAR	Has a fixed length with a maximum of 8,000 characters.
TEXT	Has storage with a variable length and a maximum of 2,127,483,647 characters or 2 GB of data.
VARCHAR	Has storage with variable length and a maximum length of 8,000 characters.
VARCHAR(max)	Has storage of variable length with a maximum of 231 characters (available for SQL Server 2005 only).

Unicode Character String

Used for Unicode characters with a maximum length established for each of the data types, although the length can be fixed or variable.

Data Type	Description
NCHAR	Has a fixed length with a maximum of 4,000 Unicode characters.
NTEXT	Has a storage of variable length with a maximum of 1 GB of Unicode data.
NVARCHAR	Has storage of variable length with a maximum of 4,000 Unicode characters.
NVARCHAR (max)	Has storage of variable length with a maximum of 231 Unicode characters.

Binary String

This data type is used to store binary data in the database with maximum lengths that can be fixed or varied. They are divided into the following:

Data Type	Description
BINARY	Has a fixed maximum length of 8,000 bytes.
IMAGE	Has a storage with variable length and a maximum size of 2 GB of data.
TEXT	Has variable storage capacity and supports a maximum length of 2,147,483,647 bytes.
VARBINARY	Has a variable storage with a maximum length of 8,000 bytes.
VARBINARY (max)	Has a variable maximum length of 231 bytes (can only be used for SQL Server 2005).

Numeric Data Types

In T-SQL, these data types are composed of eleven classifications including the possibility to store exact, approximate, integral, or decimal numbers.

Data Type	From	To
BIGINT	-9,223,372,036,854,770,000	9,223,372,036,854,770,000
BIT	1	0
DECIMAL	1E+38	$10^38 - 1$
FLOAT	-1.79E+308	1.79E+308
INT	-2,147,483,648	2,147,483,647
MONEY	-922,337,203,685,477.00	922,337,203,685,477.00
NUMERIC	1E+38	$10^38 - 1$
REAL	-3.40E+38	3.40E+38
SMALLINT	-32,768	32,767
SMALLMONEY	-214,748.36	214,748.36
TINYINT	0	255

Date and Time Data Types

Here are the six data types that can be used to store date and time in T-SQL:

Data Type	Description
DATE	Stores information in the YYYY-MM-DD format
TIME	Stores information in the HH:MM:SS:NNNNNNN format
DATETIME	Stores information in the YYYY-MM-DD HH:MM:SS:NNN format
DATETIME2	Stores information in the YYYY-MM-DD HH:MM:SS:NNNNNN format
DATETIMEOFFSET	Stores information in the YYYY-MM-DD HH:MM:SS: [.NNNNN] [+/-HH:MM] format
SMALLDATETIME	Stores information in the YYYY-MM-DD HH:MM:SS format

Miscellaneous Data Types

One of the main characteristics of T-SQL is that it has the ability to store not only spatial data types with geometric characteristics but also those with geographical characteristics. In addition to this, it can also store information in XML format and provides the user with unique data types such as CURSOR, SQL_VARIANT, TABLE, ROWVERSION, and UNIQUEIDENTIFIER.

Compatibility Between ANSI/ISO SQL and T-SQL

According to Microsoft Learn (2023), this is a table that can be used to translate the ANSI/ISO SQL data types into T-SQL and the synonyms that can be applied.

ANSI SQL	Synonym	Microsoft SQL Server Data Type
BIT, BIT VARYING	VARBINARY, BINARY VARYING BIT VARYING	BINARY, VARBINARY
DATE, TIME	DATE, TIME	DATETIME
DECIMAL	NUMERIC, DEC	DECIMAL
REAL	SINGLE, FLOAT4, IEEESINGLE	REAL
DOUBLE PRECISION, FLOAT	DOUBLE, FLOAT8, IEEEDOUBLE, NUMBER	FLOAT
SMALLINT	SHORT, INTEGER2	SMALLINT
INTEGER	LONG, INT, INTEGER4	INTEGER
INTERVAL		Not supported
CHARACTER, CHARACTER VARYING, NATIONAL CHARACTER, NATIONAL CHARACTER VARYING	TEXT(n), ALPHANUMERIC, CHARACTER, STRING, VARCHAR, CHARACTER VARYING, NCHAR, NATIONAL CHARACTER, NATIONAL CHAR, NATIONAL CHARACTER VARYING, NATIONAL CHAR VARYING (See Notes)	CHAR, VARCHAR, NCHAR, NVARCHAR

PostgreSQL Data Types

The last of the data types we are going to look at are those belonging to PostgreSQL or the PL/PgSQL dialect. Different from most of the other SQL dialects, when looking at the official documentation in PostgreSQL (2022), you will see that the data types for the language are classified into 15 different categories. This is because there is a separation between the INTEGER and the MONEY types, for example, in which both refer to numbers but are classified differently.

In this section, you are going to see each of the data types according to the classification provided by the official documentation. In addition to this, you will notice that there are some of the ANSI/ISO SQL standards that are mentioned and have the same spelling within the lists. Although they are compatible, they have different storage characteristics when compared to other databases and, therefore, they will be detailed accordingly for better understanding.

One important observation regarding PL/PgSQL is that, differently from the other dialects we have seen so far and the ANSI/ISO SQL standard, this dialect is *case-sensitive*. This means that while other RDBMSs use these data type keywords to describe the column in upper or lowercase letters, there is no difference; in PostgreSQL, this does not apply. Therefore, differently from what you have seen in the previous sections, you will see all the data type keywords expressed in lowercase, since this is the standard applied by the dialect.

All the information in this section was obtained from PostgreSQL (2022), including the tables and explanations.

Numeric Data Types

Name	Description	Range
bigint	large-range integer	-9,223,372,036,854,775,808 to +9,223,372,036,854,775,807
bigserial	large autoincrementing integer	1 to 9,223,372,036.854,775,807
decimal	user-specified precision, exact	up to 131,072 digits before the decimal point; up to 16,383 digits after the decimal point
double precision	variable-precision, inexact	15 decimal digits precision
integer	typical choice for integer	-2,147,483,648 to +2,147,483,647
numeric	user-specified precision, exact	up to 131,072 digits before the decimal point; up to 16383 digits after the decimal point
real	variable-precision, inexact	6 decimal digits precision
serial	autoincrementing integer	1 to 2,147,483,647
smallint	small-range integer	-32768 to +32,767
smallserial	small autoincrementing integer	1 to 32,767

Monetary Data Types

Name	Range
money	-92,233,720,368,547,758.08 to +92,233,720,368,547,758.07

Character Data Types

For these data types, PostgreSQL (2022), explains that "there is no performance difference among these [data] three types, apart from increased storage space when using the blank-padded type, and a few extra CPU cycles to check the length when storing into a length-constrained column."

Name	Description
character varying(n), varchar(n)	variable length with limit
character(n), char(n), bpchar(n)	fixed length, blank-padded
text	variable unlimited length

Binary Data Types

Name	Range
bytea	variable-length binary string with a size of 1 or 4 bytes plus the actual binary string

Date and Time Data Types

Name	Description
timestamp [(p)] [without time zone]	both date and time (no time zone)
timestamp[(p)] with time zone	both date and time, with time zone. Can also use the spelling abbreviation of timestamptz
date	date (no time of day)
time [(p)] [without time zone]	time of day (no date)
time [(p)] with time zone	time of day (no date), with time zone
interval [fields [(p)]	time interval

Miscellaneous Data Types

- **Enumerated data types:** used for ordered and static values.
- **Geometric:** used to represent two-dimensional spatial objects.
- **Network address:** used to store IPv4, IPv6, and MAC addresses.
- **Text search:** used to carry out full-text searches through a collection of natural-language documents. By using this

data type, it will be possible to locate the text that best matches a query.

- **JSON:** used to store data in JSON format.

Compatibility Between ANSI/ISO SQL and PL/pgSQL

These are the data types that have the same spelling and function in both ANSI/ISO SQL and PL/pgSQL (keeping in mind the use of lowercase letters):

- bigint
- bit
- bit varying
- boolean
- char
- character varying
- character
- varchar
- date
- double precision
- integer
- interval
- numeric
- decimal
- real
- smallint
- time (with or without time zone)
- timestamp (with or without time zone)
- xml

SQL Data Structures

In the previous section of this chapter, you have learned data can be stored in different formats in the database. However, just having these characteristics applied to it is not enough. The database needs to have a structure to ensure that the user can perform the queries and operations they need to. These "rules," as they can be referred to, will allow the database to understand the different instructions it is given because the information will be organized. SQL has several different data structures, and their application will depend on the type of data you are storing and how you are going to manage it.

Let's put this into a practical application. When you go grocery shopping, the supermarket offers different types of products for purchase. We could say that we have fresh products, such as fruit and vegetables, cleaning products, and pantry items, each with their own characteristics. If we were to make a comparison between these items and SQL dialects, it is possible to say that the supermarket is the database, "fruits" and "vegetables" are data types, and "apples" and "pears" are keywords of these specific data types. In addition to this, it is possible to infer that "apples" in its general sense would be ANSI/ISO SQL and their different varieties are each of the SQL dialects.

Now, what would happen if you went to the supermarket and all the fruits, vegetables, cleaning products, and pantry items were placed together, without separate aisles dedicated to a certain product category and stored without distinction of brand, type, or taking into consideration the best exposure format? In this case, finding what you want would not be impossible, but it would take a lot more time and effort to identify everything you need. The same logic can be applied to SQL data structures.

If we compared the SQL data structures to the supermarket, we could say that in addition to the consideration of the database and the data types, this information needs to be stored in an organized manner, so it is quick and easy to process and store. Just like in the supermarket, we have different aisles and areas dedicated to certain product categories, and they are each exposed in a way that they can be easily seen, the same will happen with databases.

This means that you will have an easier time managing and viewing different information when carrying out queries in an efficient manner, without the need for additional features or programs to organize what you are seeing. This provides the user with enhanced resource and service management capabilities, especially if data exchange is needed. Furthermore, organizing the data into structures gives it a reusability characteristic, saving time if you need to use the same information without the need to reorganize it. Finally, applying data structures will enable you to up or downscale the data with less effort, as well as decrease the program's processing time.

However, differently from a supermarket and its products, the data structures can be described with more than one characteristic. According to Biswal (2023), these include the following:

- Static (with fixed formats and/or sizes) or dynamic structures.
- Linear (arranging the structure in a sequential format) or nonlinear structures (in which there is no sequence).
- How much space (memory) they occupy in the database and in the device in which it is being stored.
- How much time it takes to run the queries and execute processes in the program.
- How accurately the structure information is depicted in the interface for the database being used.

As you will see further along in this section, there are several data structures the user can choose from. Deciding the best one will depend on the answer to five important questions:

1. What is the type of information (data type) you are going to store?
2. How is the information going to be used?
3. Where is the data going to be stored?
4. What is the most efficient way to organize this data so it is easily understood?
5. What data structure will provide the optimal storage in the device so that the processing is not time-consuming?

In addition to answering these questions, it is essential to identify the operations that will be carried out and check if these are supported by the selected structure. Suppose you are going to use arithmetic operations with the data such as adding and subtracting numbers. In this case, the data types need to be numeric, and the selected structure must support the operations, as opposed to being stored as a graph, for example.

Now that you know what to look for in a data structure, let's see what the different structures are available in SQL, what they can be used for, and their main characteristics.

Data Structure Types

Data structures can be classified into three different categories: static or dynamic, linear or nonlinear, and homogeneous or heterogeneous. While there is a clear difference between the first two categories, the last can be applied to all of them, in which the homogeneous structures will consist of values that have the same data type and heterogeneous of those that have varied data types.

For a clear understanding, the different SQL structures have been divided in this section into linear, nonlinear, and table data structure types.

Linear Data Structures

When you have a linear data structure, this means that the data will be arranged in a sequence that links the element to the one that comes before and after it. In these data structures, there is no hierarchy between the data and the relationship between them has only one form. In SQL, the linear data structures are divided as follows:

- **Array:** The simplest of the data structure forms, consists of elements that have the same data type grouped.
- **Linked list:** Stores the elements of a list (collection) in a linear order, in which each item is linked to the subsequent one belonging to the same list.
- **Queue:** This data structure organizes the elements in a collection in a linear order, in which the concept of first-in, first-out (FIFO) is applied to the operations.
- **Stack:** Similar to a queue data structure, in a stack the collection is placed in a linear order in which both the concepts FIFO and last-in, first-out (LIFO) can be applied to the operations.

Nonlinear Data Structures

In nonlinear data structures, the elements do not have a linear sequence but are linked in a hierarchical manner to one or more items. This means they can have several layers that connect to each other. The two types of nonlinear data structures available in SQL are:

- **Graph:** In this data structure, the database tables will be represented in an image by using a variety of nodes and edges. SQL supports different types of graphs to visualize the data.
- **Tree:** When using trees to structure data, you will have a single root value that will be divided into leaf nodes, each associated with a specific value. This is an ideal approach to visualize data with multiple levels and a specific hierarchy. Similarly to the graphs, there are different varieties of trees that can be applied to the database.

Table Data Structures

As the name suggests, when you have these types of data structures, they will be visualized in a table format. These are the different table structure types available in SQL:

- **Hash table:** This is a table that stores data in a key-value format in which the key acts as an index for the elements stored.
- **Heap table:** In this type of table, no index is used, which means that the data is randomly stored and considers the first available space to enter new data.
- **Partitioned table:** The data in these tables will be divided into small groups or files that enable the user to easily manage the information.
- **System table:** This table is generally used for metadata storage that will be applied server-wide.
- **Temporary table:** When the user wants to share data for a short time, this is the table that can be used with connections that can be local or global.
- **Wide table:** Consists of a table that can have up to 30,000 columns. Each column will have a definition and a variable

assigned to it.

SQL Operators

Once you have the SQL data types and structures learned and acknowledged, it is time to see how these can interact with each other. In the case of SQL, it has what are called "operators," which are a list of symbols that will help the user perform computations with the data in the database. These operations are mainly mathematical and logical, and are usually divided into three categories:

- arithmetic operators
- comparison operators
- logical operators.

These operators can be used to have different data values interact with each other. Here are three lists with the operators belonging to each of the categories and their applications.

Arithmetic Operators

Operator	Description
-	Used to subtract element values
*	Used to multiply element values
/	Used to divide element values and is used with the keyword "ALL"
+	Used to add element values
%	Used to get the remainder result of when an element is divided by another

Comparison Operators

Operator	Description
<	Less than
>	Greater than
=	Equal to
<=	Less than or equal to
>=	Greater than or equal to
<>	Not equal to

Logical Operators

Operator	Description
NOT	Analyzes a single Boolean argument and changes from TRUE to FALSE or from FALSE to TRUE
AND	Compares two Boolean expressions and will have TRUE as the output only if they both fulfill this condition
OR	Compares two Boolean expressions and will have TRUE as the output if one of them has this condition

SQL still has other operators that are not considered to be a part of any of these categories. They include ALL, ANY, and, BETWEEN, for example, among others. The use of these operators is not as usual as the ones you have just seen and can be replaced by using a longer syntax.

Quick Overview

To make your understanding and referencing easier when comparing each of the SQL dialects for the mentioned databases, here is a list that compares the data types and their application in each RDBMS by category:

Character Data Types

Data Type	Oracle	MySQL	MS SQL Server	PostgreSQL
BINARY	-	Yes	Yes	-
BINARY VARYING	-	-	Yes	-
BLOB	Yes	Yes	-	-
BYTEA	-	-	-	Yes
CHAR	Yes	Yes	Yes	Yes
CHARACTER	Yes	-	-	Yes
CHARACTER VARYING	Yes	-	Yes	Yes
CLOB	Yes	-	-	-
ENUM	-	Yes	-	Yes
LONG	Yes	-	-	-
LONG RAW	Yes	-	-	-
LONGBLOB	-	Yes	-	-
LONGTEXT	-	Yes	-	-
MEDIUMBLOB	-	Yes	-	-
MEDIUMTEXT	-	Yes	-	-
NCHAR	Yes	-	Yes	-
NCLOB	Yes	-	-	-
NTEXT	-	-	Yes	-
NVARCHAR	-	-	Yes	-
NVARCHAR2	Yes	-	-	-
RAW	Yes	-	-	-
SET	-	Yes	-	-
TEXT	-	Yes	Yes	Yes
TINYBLOB	-	Yes	-	-
TINYTEXT	-	Yes	-	-
VARBINARY	-	Yes	-	-
VARCHAR	Yes	Yes	Yes	Yes
VARCHAR2	Yes	-	-	-

Numeric Data Types

Data Type	Oracle	MySQL	MS SQL Server	PostgreSQL
BIGINT	-	Yes	Yes	Yes
BIGSERIAL	-	-	-	Yes
BINARY_DOUBLE	Yes	-	-	-
BINARY_FLOAT	Yes	-	-	-
BIT	-	Yes	Yes	-
DEC	-	Yes	Yes	-
DECIMAL	Yes	Yes	Yes	Yes
DOUBLE	-	Yes	-	-
DOUBLE PRECISION	Yes	Yes	Yes	Yes
FIXED	-	Yes	-	-
FLOAT	Yes	Yes	Yes	-
INT	Yes	Yes	Yes	-
INTEGER	Yes	Yes	Yes	Yes
MEDIUMINT	-	Yes	-	-
MONEY	-	-	Yes	Yes
NUMBER	Yes	-	-	-
NUMERIC	Yes	Yes	Yes	Yes
REAL	Yes	Yes	Yes	Yes
SERIAL	-	-	-	Yes
SMALLINT	Yes	Yes	Yes	Yes
SMALLMONEY	-	-	Yes	-
SMALLSERIAL	-	-	-	Yes
TINYINT	-	Yes	Yes	-

Date and Time Data Types

Data Type	Oracle	MySQL	MS SQL Server	PostgreSQL
DATE	Yes	Yes	Yes	Yes
DATETIME	-	Yes	Yes	-
DATETIME2	-	-	Yes	-
DATETIMEOFF SET	-	-	Yes	-
INTERVAL	-	-	-	Yes
INTERVAL DAY TO SECOND	Yes	-	-	-
INTERVAL YEAR TO MONTH	Yes	-	-	-
SMALLDATETI ME	-	-	Yes	-
TIME	-	Yes	Yes	Yes
TIME WITH TIME ZONE	-	-	-	Yes
TIMESTAMP	Yes	Yes	-	Yes
TIMESTAMP WITH LOCAL TIME ZONE	Yes	-	-	-
TIMESTAMP WITH TIME ZONE	Yes	-	-	Yes
YEAR	-	Yes	-	-

Now that you know all the data types that can be used for each of the most used RDBMS, it is time to learn how to manage the database. In the next chapter, you will be introduced to the basic SQL techniques to carry out queries and commands and understand functionalities. These will be the base of your learning and will enable you to understand the subsequent chapters, in which you will be taught intermediate and advanced techniques. All of these will be applied in the end, when you will develop your own project and put your knowledge to use.

Chapter 4
Basic SQL Techniques

For the last three chapters, you have read about SQL basic structures, information, characteristics, operators, and applications. While having a foundation in the language is the best place to start, it is useless if you do not know how to use it. Therefore, starting with this chapter and for the following two, you will be taught some of the basic, intermediate, and advanced SQL techniques that can be applied to your own program. This first chapter will provide the basic commands you should know before advancing to more complex or intricate techniques.

Regardless of how the database will be used, knowing the basic SQL commands will help prepare you to perform more complex operations. This knowledge will be applied to the most diverse industries, from data science and healthcare to marketing and financial businesses—sometimes, the most basic instruction will bring you the results you need. At the end of the chapter, you will be given 10 exercises to practice and test your knowledge of the information provided in this chapter.

Command vs. Query

The first thing that is essential to learn is that there are two different actions that can be carried out in SQL databases: commands and queries. Although they have the same performance and one does not have an advantage over the other, the main difference between these is that in the query, you will not be modifying the database structure or status, while in commands, this is possible. To put it simply, when you carry out a command, it will modify the state of the database while when you carry out a query, you will be reading the information it contains.

SQL Commands and Syntax

SQL commands are used to create tables, add, modify, or delete information, and manage users who will have access to it. These can be classified into the following five categories, each with its own set of commands:

1. DDL—Data Definition Language: The commands in this category are used to create or modify the structure of a database and the elements it contains. These are the commands belonging to this category:

- **Alter:** used to modify the structure of a database.
- **Comment:** used to add comments to the database.
- **Create:** used to create a database, table, or its elements.
- **Drop:** used to delete a database, table, or its elements.
- **Rename:** used to rename an element in the database.
- **Truncate:** used to delete all the data and elements from a table in the database.

One interesting fact about these commands is that four of them make up the *CRUD* acronym, which represents the commands CREATE, READ (SELECT), UPDATE, and DELETE and is frequently adopted in the SQL community.

2. DQL—Data Query Language: The command in this category is used to perform queries on the data contained in the database. Is composed of only one command, "select."

3. DML—Data Manipulation Language: The commands in this category are used to manipulate the data and elements contained in the database and are usually applied together with those belonging to the DCL statements. The commands belonging to this category are:

- **Call:** used to call a subprogram belonging to Java or PL/SQL.
- **Delete:** used to delete all the records from the database table.
- **Explain plan:** used to describe what the access path to the data is.
- **Insert:** used to add new tables to the database.
- **Lock:** used to create table control in the database.

4. DCL—Data Control Language: These commands are used to control access to the database, including the application of restrictions, permissions, and other control features. The two commands belonging to this category are:

- **Grant:** used to give access and privileges to the database.
- **Revoke:** used to withdraw access and privileges to the database.

5. TCL—Transaction Control Language: These last set of commands are used to group different tasks into one and are used to control how the transaction will be executed. These are the commands part of this category:

- **Begin:** used to start a transaction.
- **Commit:** used to commit a transaction.
- **Rollback:** used to undo a transaction in case there are any errors.
- **Savepoint:** used to save a certain action in a transaction.

You might be wondering how these are used and the syntax that should be applied, and that is understandable. However, you should not worry, since their syntax structure and applications will be given further along in this chapter. In the meantime, let's take a look into what SQL queries and what they can do.

SQL Queries

When you carry out a query in SQL, it means that you are looking to obtain the data contained in the database according to a certain specification. This means you can ask it to perform a calculation, answer a question, combine data, or several other possibilities. It is important to remember that when queries are carried out, there will be no modification in the database structure or data.

Using queries enables you to easily find information within a database, especially when there is a lot of information to manage and sort through. This means that instead of having to scroll through a list, you can use the statements provided by SQL to ask the database to perform an action. This is such a powerful way of finding and managing data that major companies such as Spotify, Facebook, Google, and Amazon use it to manage their databases.

Basic SQL Commands and Queries

Now that you have read about commands and queries, let's see how and when they can be used, their syntax, and examples. Three tables have been created for you to use as reference and for a better understanding of the examples.

Database Name
Supermarket
Bank
Store
Auto_shop

"Goodie Supermarket" Database

Database Tables
Employees
Sales
Fruit
Vegetables

"Employee" table

ID	Name	Shift	Start Time	End Time
1	John Smith	Morning	2023-01-29 08:30:25	2023-01-29 14:30:01
5	Carrie Jones	Afternoon	2023-01-29 08:32:27	2023-01-29 15:27:15
7	Sam Davidson	Afternoon	2023-01-29 13:00:07	2023-01-29 20:03:33
9	Summer Clark	Evening	2023-01-29 21:35:56	2023-01-29 02:15:49

"Fruit" table

ID	Name	Price
1405	Apple	0.50
1406	Banana	0.87
1407	Pear	0.33
1408	Pineapple	0.68

Here are the commands and queries you should apply to this database and its tables:

Create database: Used to create a new database.

- **Syntax:**

```
CREATE DATABASE db_name;
```

- **Example:** Create a database for a candy store.

```
CREATE DATABASE candy_store;
```

Use database: Used to define the database you will use.

- **Syntax:**

```
USE db_name;
```

- **Example:** Write a syntax for using the supermarket database.

```
USE supermarket;
```

Drop database: Used to delete a database.

- **Syntax:**

```
DROP DATABASE db_name;
```

- **Example:** Delete the auto_shop database.

```
DROP DATABASE auto_shop
```

Exhibit database: Used to show all the available databases.

- **Syntax:**

```
SHOW DATABASES
```

Show tables in database: Used to show all the tables contained in a certain database.

- **Syntax:**

```
SHOW TABLES
```

Create table: Used to create a table in a database.

- **Syntax:**

```
CREATE TABLE table_name (
Column_1 datatype,
Column_2 datatype,
);
```

- **Example:** Create a table in the supermarket database that will include the total earned per day.

```
CREATE TABLE income (
Day DATE,
Total MONEY,
);
```

Delete from table: Used to delete all the records from the table in the database. Should be used with WHERE to specify what you want to delete.

- **Syntax:**

```
DELETE FROM table_name;
```

- **Example:** Delete the evening shift from the employee table.

```
DELETE FROM employee
WHERE shift = 'evening';
```

Alter table: Used to change the structure of a table.

- **Syntax:**

```
ALTER TABLE table_name;
ADD column_name datatype;
```

- **Example:** Insert an extra column in the employees' table with the name "salary."

```
ALTER TABLE employees
ADD salary MONEY;
```

Drop table: Used to delete a table in the database.

- **Syntax:**

```
DROP TABLE table_name;
```

- **Example:** Exclude the vegetable table from the database and ask the program to show all available tables.

```
DROP TABLE vegetables;
SHOW TABLES
```

Select: Used to select the information you want from a database. Used in association with "FROM" to indicate the table in which it can be found. Will be used with other queries in more advanced coding.

- **Syntax:**

```
SELECT items
FROM table;
```

- **Example:** In this example, we want to select the fruit and their prices from the fruit table.

```
SELECT name, price
FROM Fruit;
```

Another syntax that can be used with SELECT, but will be applied when you want to select all the data in the table is to use the syntax with an asterisk (*):

```
SELECT * FROM fruit;
```

Where: Is used to determine the location while limiting the number of rows you want this information from. Can be used with the keywords LIKE, BETWEEN, AND, IN, or OR.

- **Syntax:**

```
SELECT items
FROM table
WHERE place;
```

- **Example:** In this example, we want to select only apples and pears and their prices from the fruit table.

```
SELECT name, price
FROM Fruit
WHERE (ID = 1405 AND 1407);
```

Order by: Used to place the elements of a table in ascending (default) or descending order.

- **Syntax:**

```
SELECT column1, column2,
FROM table_name
ORDER BY column1, column2, ASC;
```

- **Example:** Order the names of the employees in the employee table in descending alphabetical order.

```
SELECT *,
FROM employee
ORDER BY name DESC;
```

In this case, we will need to select the whole table so all the data is equally ordered.

Insert into: Used to insert information into a database table.

- **Syntax:**

```
INSERT INTO table_name
VALUES (value1, value2, value3,...);
```

- **Example:** Insert into the table "fruit" a new product ID, name, and price.

```
INSERT INTO fruit
VALUES (1409, 'lemon', 0.21);
```

Update: Used to update an element in a specific table. Should be used in association with "WHERE" to determine the location of the element that will be modified.

- **Syntax:**

```
UPDATE table_name
SET column1 = value1,
column2 = value2, …
WHERE condition;
```

- **Example:** In this example, we want to modify the shift that Sam Davidson, with ID number 07 works in from the afternoon to the evening. This information is located in the employee table.

```
UPDATE Employee
SET Shift= "Evening"
WHERE Id = 7;
```

Comments: Used to explain part of the statements or the query that is being made. If placed in this format, it will not be processed along with the code.

- **Syntax:**

One-line comment:
```
- place your comment
(code)
- place another comment
(code)
```
Multiline comment:
```
(code)
/*start the comment here
and finish it or add another here*/
(Code)
```
In-line comment:
```
(code) /*write a comment here*/
```

There you have it! These are the basic commands and queries that you should know how to use in SQL to start managing your database. To ensure that you have learned them and to practice your new skill, you will find in the next section of this chapter a list of exercises you should apply to the provided tables.

Exercises

Tables

Databases

Database Name
7th_grade
8th_grade
9th_grade
10th_grade
11th_grade
12th_grade

"Class" Database

Database Tables
English
Math
Chemistry
Biology
Spanish
Physics
Economy
History
Teachers

"Chemistry" table

ID	First_name	Last_name	Final_grade	Period
1	John	Harrison	C	1
5	Mary	Garcia	A	1
7	Calvin	Home	D	4
9	Summer	Scott	F	6
15	Joy	Sing	B+	3
26	David	Wu	C-	2
27	Richard	Sky	A+	5
51	Alice	Davies	A-	2

"Teacher" table

ID	Name	Class
1586	Craig Jones	History
1597	Samantha Child	English
1523	Erick Shone	Chemistry
1478	Gabriela Santos	Spanish
1365	Philip Klein	Physics

Questions

1. Create a database to store the information of all the students in the school and ask the program to show you all available databases.
2. Add a table to the "class" database with the name "active_students" with the following information: first name, middle name, last name, date of birth, age, and address.
3. Add a column to the teacher table to include their salary.
4. Select the grades from all the students who have chemistry.

5. Select all the information available in the "teacher" table.
6. Order all the students attending chemistry in alphabetical order.
7. Insert in the teacher table a new art teacher with the name of Gary Ford, ID number 1600.
8. Update the chemistry grade for Summer Scott from an F to a B-.
9. Delete Gabriela Santos as the Spanish teacher.
10. Select all the students who attend chemistry after 1st period and before 6th period.

Answer Key

1.

```
CREATE DATABASE students;
SHOW DATABASES;
```

2.

```
CREATE TABLE active_students (
first_name CHAR,
middle_name CHAR,
last_name CHAR,
dob DATE,
age INT,
address CHAR
);
```

3.

```
ALTER TABLE employees
ADD salary MONEY;
```

4.

```
SELECT grade
FROM chemistry;
```

5.

```
SELECT * FROM teachers;
```

6.

```
SELECT *
FROM chemistry
ORDER BY last_name ASC;
```

7.

```
INSERT INTO teacher
VALUES (1600, 'Gary Ford', 'Art')
```

8.

```
UPDATE chemistry
SET grade = 'B-'
WHERE id = 9
```

9.

```
DELETE FROM teachers
WHERE name = 'Gabriela Santos'
```

10.

```
SELECT first_name, last name
FROM chemistry
WHERE period > 1 AND period < 6;
```

Did you get them right? If not, please feel encouraged to go back and look for clarification in the explanation to see what you might have missed. If you have gotten all the answers correct, congratulations! You are now ready to move on to more elaborate SQL techniques, which will be seen in the next chapter. If you are ready, read on!

Take a Brief Pause

"Put knowledge where people trip over it."

— Carla O'Dell

At this stage of your reading journey, you're steeped in knowledge about the pillars upon which SQL stands—from the characteristics that make this language so useful for databases to dialects, databases, and data types. I hope you are feeling more confident about SQL and agree that it's a far more graspable language than its fame would indicate.

SQL certainly isn't going anywhere. Despite being developed in the 1970s as a means to retrieve information from relational databases, it is still the pillar upon which modern data management and interpretation is based. New languages may come and go, but SQL is currently the most widely used and dependable. If you are keen on furthering your career in database management, analysis, or development (to name just a few areas), it should definitely be high on your priority list.

In this book, I aim to provide clear, concise explanations of the SQL language and its many applications so that you can effectively cope with issues that crop up when you create or manage databases. As intricate as SQL can seem, even someone with little to no experience in languages can retrieve and understand data and pose the right queries.

If this book inspires and motivates you to deepen your knowledge of SQL, I hope you can provide hope and a sense of direction for other readers who fear that SQL is too inherently complex to master.

By leaving a review of this book on Amazon, you can show others where to find the information they seek in an easy-to-understand, logical format.

Simply by telling them how this book has shaped your understanding of SQL, you'll help them discover that SQL isn't the exclusive realm of computer engineers or those who are already tech whizzes.

Thank you for your support. Let's move on and immerse ourselves more deeply into SQL techniques.

Scan the QR code below

Chapter 5
Intermediate SQL Techniques

After you have mastered the basics of SQL, it is time to move forward and learn some techniques that can be classified as "intermediate." While it is essential to know how to create a database and tables and modify the information available, SQL provides the user with many more features than what you have seen so far. Some of these techniques include joining tables and information, creating indexes, and aggregating information.

This chapter provides you with intermediate command and query techniques you should know before advancing to the final step of the process, which is learning advanced techniques in SQL. As you read the content available in the following sections, you will see that SQL provides features that will make managing and using RDBMS versatile and flexible, adjusting to your business needs. As usual, once you are done with the content, you will be provided with exercises to ensure you have retained the knowledge and that you can put these techniques into practice.

Intermediate SQL Commands and Queries

Although learning more complex techniques of using SQL in RDBMS might sound intimidating, you will notice that all the information that has been provided to you so far will be a great support to help you develop this skill. In this section, you are going to learn intermediate commands and queries that can be used in all types of databases. To enhance the learning process, as was done in the previous chapter, you will be provided with the application, syntax, and example of how these can be used. To illustrate the given examples, three tables will be provided to be used as reference.

"Quantity" table

Year	Product	Kilograms
2021	Soybeans	57,687,125
2021	Maize	32,458,234
2021	Wheat	15,458,988
2021	Sugar	10,879,267
2020	Soybeans	63,875,965
2020	Maize	28,227,394
2020	Wheat	12,478,932
2020	Sugar	9,785,236
2019	Soybeans	51,549,853
2019	Maize	30,582,718
2019	Wheat	13,782,961
2019	Sugar	5,851,369

"Destination" table

Year	Product	Countries
2021	Soybeans	Spain, Germany
2021	Maize	Portugal, Belgium
2021	Wheat	France, Netherlands
2021	Sugar	Belgium, Italy
2020	Soybeans	France, Spain
2020	Maize	Belgium, Portugal
2020	Wheat	France, Spain
2020	Sugar	Italy, Spain
2019	Soybeans	France, Netherlands
2019	Maize	Spain, Belgium
2019	Wheat	Spain, France
2019	Sugar	Portugal, Italy

"Origin" Table

Year	Product	Place
2021	Soybeans	United States
2021	Maize	Brazil
2021	Wheat	Argentina
2021	Sugar	Brazil
2020	Soybeans	Argentina
2020	Maize	United States
2020	Wheat	Uruguay
2020	Sugar	Brazil
2019	Soybeans	United States
2019	Maize	Brazil
2019	Wheat	Argentina
2019	Sugar	India

"Produced" table

Year	Product	Country	Amount
2021	Soybeans	United States	86,000,000
2021	Maize	Brazil	47,000,000
2021	Wheat	Argentina	23,000,000
2021	Sugar	Brazil	10,879,267
2020	Soybeans	Argentina	63,875,965
2020	Maize	United States	30,000,000
2020	Wheat	Uruguay	12,478,932
2020	Sugar	Brazil	9,785,236
2019	Soybeans	United States	51,549,853
2019	Maize	Brazil	40,000,000
2019	Wheat	Argentina	20,000,000
2019	Sugar	India	10,000,000

Create index: Used to create an index on the table, making the information easier to find.

- **Syntax:**

```
CREATE INDEX index_name
ON table_name (column_name);
```

- **Example:** Create an index for the weight of products imported per year.

```
CREATE INDEX weight
ON quantity (kilograms);
```

Drop index: Used to delete an index on the table.

- **Syntax:**

```
DROP INDEX index_name;
```

Example: Drop an index for the weight of products imported per year.

```
DROP INDEX weight;
```

Aggregate function: Works as an aggregate function that uses COUNT, MIN, MAX, AVG, and SUM to group the results of a data set in a table.

- **Syntax:**

```
SELECT function (column_name) AS
"new_column_name"
FROM table_name;
```

- **Example 1:** Add the total weight of all the products imported between the years of 2019 and 2022.

```
SELECT SUM (kilograms) AS "Total_Imported"
FROM quantity;
```

- **Example 2:** Find the maximum product weight imported between the years of 2019 and 2022.

```
SELECT MAX (kilograms) AS "Maximum_weight"
FROM quantity;
```

Count: Is an aggregate function used to count the number of times that a record appears in a table.

- **Syntax:**

```
SELECT COUNT (*) AS "new_column_name"
FROM table_name
WHERE column_name = what_you_want_-
to_count;
```

- **Example:** Count for how many years the product "maize" has been imported.

```
SELECT COUNT (*) AS "Years_Importing"
FROM countries
WHERE product = 'Maize'
```

Distinct: Is a clause that can be added to your statement so that the only records that are returned to you are those that are unique. It can be used as a stand-alone clause or in association with "COUNT."

- **Syntax:**

```
SELECT DISTINCT column_name
FROM table_name;
```

- **Example 1:** Count how many distinct destination combinations are in the table.

```
SELECT DISTINCT AS "Destination"
FROM destination;
```

- **Example 2:** Count how many distinct products have been imported.

```
SELECT COUNT (DISTINCT product) AS
"Different_Products"
FROM destination;
```

Group by: Works as an aggregate function to group the data set into different records by using functions.

- **Syntax:**

```
SELECT column
FUNCTION (column_name) AS new_column_name
FROM table_name
WHERE specify condition
GROUP BY category;
```

- **Example:** Calculate the average, maximum, and minimum weights per type of product imported since 2019.

```
SELECT product
MAX (weight) AS "Maximum_Quantity",
MIN (weight) AS "Minimum_Quantity",
AVG (weight) AS "Average_Quantity"
FROM quantity
WHERE year >= 2019
GROUP BY product;
```

Having: When you apply the having clause, you are using an extra filter to sort the information that has been given to you in the GROUP BY feature. It is usually used to substitute the WHERE clause, since they are not allowed in this instance.

- **Syntax:**

```
SELECT column
FUNCTION (column_name) AS new_column_name
FROM table_name
GROUP BY category
HAVING FUNCTION (column name) clause;
```

- **Example:** Suppose you want to identify the years in which less than 10,000,000 kilos of products was bought. For this calculation, you would use "HAVING" since you are going to apply a condition to the quantity you want.

```
SELECT year
SUM (weight) AS Total_imported
FROM quantity
GROUP BY year
HAVING SUM (weight) < 10000000;
```

Inner join: Is used when you want to combine rows from two tables with identical column names, even if the data is different. An important detail to notice is that this feature only supports *one* column. The common column will be specified by using the "ON" clause. Only the rows with an exact match will bring a result.

- **Syntax:**

```
SELECT comma_separated_column_names
FROM table_1
INNER JOIN table_2 ON condition
table1.common_column = table_2
common_column;
```

- **Example:** Suppose you want to join the information in the "Destination" table with the data in the "Origin" table to create a single table displaying both the origin and destination of products. In this example, the "year" and "product" columns are common to both tables.

/*Notice that for this code you will need to add the column names in the tables because the columns have the same name*/

```
SELECT destination.year, destination.prod-
uct, origin.place AS origin, destination.-
countries AS destination
FROM destination
INNER JOIN origin ON destination.year =
origin.year AND destination.product =
origin.product;
```

Left outer join: Known as a variety of the "outer join" function, will return as a result from the query only the rows that *do not match* from the *left* table and the rows that *match* from both tables. If there is no match, the value will be filled in the table as NULL.

- **Syntax:**

```
SELECT comma_separated_column_names
FROM table1
LEFT OUTER JOIN table2 ON table1.common_-
column = table2.common_column;
```

- **Example:** Using LEFT OUTER JOIN, write the code for the products that were produced in a specific year (e.g., 2021) but not exported in that same year. Additionally, for each of these products, determine the country where they were produced.

/*Since the columns have the same names, we will once again distinguish between them as you can see in the code*/

```
--"p" is being used to identify the
produced table
-- "q" is being used to identify the quan-
tity table
SELECT p.Product, p.Year, p.Country
FROM Produced AS p
/* use LEFT OUTER JOIN to combine both
tables based on the similar columns*/
LEFT OUTER JOIN Quantity AS q ON p.Product
= q.Product AND p.Year = q.Year
-- use WHERE to filter the results for the
rows that do not match quantity
WHERE q.Kilograms IS NULL;
```

Once this query is performed, it will return the desired result: products produced in a specific year but not exported in the same year, along with their corresponding product, year, and country of production.

Right outer join: Also known as a variety of the "outer join" function, will return as a result from the query only the rows that *do not match* from the *right* table and the rows that *match* from both tables.

- **Syntax:**

```
SELECT comma_separated_column_names
FROM table1
RIGHT OUTER JOIN table2 ON table1.common_-
column = table2.common_column;
```

- **Example:** Using the "Quantity" and "Produced" tables,
  retrieve the products that were produced in a specific year
  (2021) but not exported in that same year. Additionally, for
  each of these products, determine the country where they
  were produced.

```
SELECT p.Product, p.Year, p.Country
FROM Quantity AS q
RIGHT OUTER JOIN Produced AS p
ON q.Product = p.Product AND q.Year =
p.Year
WHERE q.Kilograms IS NULL;
```

Here, you might believe that there is no difference between what
you have seen in the LEFT and the RIGHT OUTER JOIN.
However, you should note that there is a significant difference
between these techniques.

In the first example, using LEFT OUTER JOIN, all records from
the "Produced" table were preserved and added to the "Quantity"
table the matching records. If any of the records in the "Produced"
table do not match the ones in the "Quantity" table, they will have
as an output the NULL result.

On the other hand, when we consider the second example using
the RIGHT OUTER JOIN, all records from the "Quantity" table
were used and included the records that matched with those in the

"Produced" table. All the records in the "Quantity" table that do not have a match in the "Produced" table will present NULL values in the columns from the "Produced" table.

Essentially speaking, this means that the difference between both techniques is that in a LEFT OUTER JOIN, you keep all records from the left table and matching records from the right table, while in a RIGHT OUTER JOIN, you keep all records from the right table and matching records from the left table. When you are carrying out a SQL query, your choice between LEFT and RIGHT OUTER JOIN will depend on which table's records you want to ensure are present in the result set, despite the matches that might be presented in the output.

Full outer join: The other variety of the "outer join" function, will return as a result of the query all the rows that *do not match* and those that *match* from both tables.

- **Syntax:**

```
SELECT comma_separated_column_names
FROM table1
FULL OUTER JOIN table2 ON table1.common_-
column = table2.common_column;
```

- **Example:** Identify a combined list of products and their corresponding quantities from the "Quantity" table and products with their production years from the "Produced" table. The new tables must show the product name, kilograms (from "Quantity"), and production year (from "Produced") and all rows should be included in the output.

```
SELECT Product, Kilograms, Year_produced
FROM Quantity
FULL OUTER JOIN Produced ON
Quantity.Product = Produced.Product;
```

Multiple join: As the name might suggest, when you use the "MULTIPLE JOIN" query, you are going to combine two or more tables that have the same information. This type of join will normally be used when you have information that is used more than once in different tables.

- **Syntax:**

```
SELECT comma_separated_column_names
FROM first_table_alias
JOIN second_table_alias ON join_condi-
tion_for_second_table
JOIN third_table_alias ON join_condition_-
for_third_table
-- Include as many JOIN clauses as needed
WHERE condition;
```

- **Example:** You want to join all the information that is available in the tables for the year 2021. Join the information about products, their production, export, and destination countries for this year.

```
SELECT p.Product, o.Place AS "Production
Country", q.Kilograms AS "Exported
Kilograms", d.Countries AS "Destination
Countries"
FROM Produced AS p
```

```
JOIN Quantity AS q ON p.Product =
q.Product AND p.Year = q.Year
JOIN Destination AS d ON p.Product =
d.Product AND p.Year = d.Year
JOIN Origin AS o ON p.Product = o.Product
AND p.Year = o.Year
WHERE p.Year = 2021;
```

Views: When the developer uses the "VIEWS" feature, they are using a form of virtual table that shows the full table that is on the database or only a partial image of what is there. There are three types of VIEW that can be used in SQL: CREATE VIEW, DROP VIEW, and ALTER VIEW. This item will explore these three uses subsequently for easier comprehension.

- **Syntax CREATE VIEW:**

```
-- view_name will be the name you want to
give to the view
CREATE VIEW view_name AS
SELECT column1, column2.....
- table_name is the table that will
provide the data
FROM table_name
WHERE condition;
```

- **Syntax DROP VIEW:**

```
DROP VIEW view_name;
```

- **Syntax ALTER VIEW:**

```
ALTER VIEW view_name AS
SELECT column1, column2.....
FROM table_name
WHERE condition;
```

- **Example:** Suppose you only want to look into the information of the exported quantity of product for the year 2021. You should use the quantity table to obtain this information and then change it to 2020. You should create the view, alter it, and then drop it after you are no longer using it.

CREATE VIEW
```
CREATE VIEW ExportedQuantity AS
SELECT Product, Kilograms
FROM Quantity
WHERE Year = 2021;
```

ALTER VIEW
```
ALTER VIEW ExportedQuantity AS
SELECT Product, Kilograms
FROM Quantity
WHERE Year = 2020;
```

DROP VIEW
```
DROP VIEW ExportedQuantity;
```

UNION (ALL): Differently from the JOIN functions, which are used to combine two different data sets belonging to different tables, SQL also has the "UNION" function, which enables the user to combine the results from different SELECT statements. In this case, there are options that can be used: "UNION" and "UNION ALL." The main difference between both of these queries is that in the UNION statement, all the duplicates will be eliminated while in the UNION ALL statement, the duplicates will be maintained.

- **Syntax UNION:** SELECT column1, column2, ...

```
FROM table1
UNION
SELECT column1, column2, ...
FROM table2;
```

- **UNION ALL:** SELECT column1, column2, ...

```
FROM table1
UNION ALL
SELECT column1, column2, ...
FROM table2;
```

- **Example:** Suppose you want to create a list of all unique products that were either exported (from "Quantity" table) or produced (from "Produced" table) in 2021, but also include products produced in 2021 according to the "Origin" table. For these cases, you would use either UNION or UNION ALL, depending on if you wanted or not the information to be duplicated.

UNION:
```
SELECT Product
FROM Quantity
WHERE Year = 2021
UNION
SELECT Product
```

```
FROM Produced
WHERE Year = 2021
UNION
SELECT Product
FROM Origin
WHERE Year = 2021;
```

UNION ALL:
```
SELECT Product
FROM Quantity
WHERE Year = 2021
UNION ALL
SELECT Product
FROM Produced
WHERE Year = 2021
UNION ALL
SELECT Product
FROM Origin
WHERE Year = 2021;
```

Minus (Except): When you use the "MINUS" operator (in PL/SQL) or "EXCEPT" (in other databases), you are going to subtract the result of a second table from a first table. This means that the statement will only bring back to the user the rows that are unique between the selected table and the table to which it is being compared.

- **Syntax:**

```
SELECT column1, column2, ... columnN
FROM table_name
WHERE condition
EXCEPT
```

```
SELECT column1, column2, ... columnN
FROM table_name
WHERE condition;
```

- **Example:** Let's use as an illustration of this technique a situation in which you are going to find products that were produced in 2021 (from the "Produced" table) but were not exported in the same year (from the "Quantity" table).

```
SELECT Product
FROM Produced
WHERE Year = 2021
EXCEPT
SELECT Product
FROM Quantity
WHERE Year = 2021;
```

A Few Words

As you learn new skills and techniques to use SQL in an RDBMS, you will see that there are different solutions that can be applied to the same problem. However, using the best approach will depend on how you structure your question and what are the results you are looking for. To ensure that you have the best results, here are a few things you should keep in mind to make the best use of your database.

- Be clear on what is the question that you want to answer.
- Understand how the database and the data are structured.
- Identify if you have the appropriate data to answer the question efficiently.
- Study the queries you want to carry out and understand the rationale before applying it.

- Look into different ways that you can query the available data to extract the most useful information possible.
- Map your query possibilities according to the data you have.
- Once you start applying queries, test as many variations as possible to ensure you have a complete view of all the outcome possibilities.
- Study new ways to apply SQL and learn different techniques.
- Practice as much as you can!

By following these few tips, you will very likely enhance your abilities in applying the SQL skills you have learned so far and those you will still learn in this book. Now, to ensure that you have understood and retained what was taught in this chapter, continue to the next section to practice your intermediate SQL techniques with a few exercises.

Exercises

Here are 10 practice exercises to help you train your intermediate SQL techniques. Please use the three available tables as references for the query and command statement construction.

Tables

"Model" table

Model	Color	Units_Sold
Camaro	Yellow	150
Camaro	Black	75
Camaro	Red	100
Corolla	Black	500
Corolla	Silver	750
Corolla	Gold	225
Corolla	White	85
Mustang	Black	145
Mustang	Silver	60
Focus	Silver	750
Focus	Black	1000
Focus	Burgundy	550
Accord	Silver	320
Accord	Black	460

"Produced" table

Model	Color	Units_Produced
Camaro	Yellow	200
Camaro	Black	150
Camaro	Red	100
Corolla	Black	515
Corolla	Silver	800
Corolla	Gold	240
Corolla	White	85
Mustang	Black	150
Mustang	Silver	60
Focus	Silver	870
Focus	Black	2000
Focus	Burgundy	1500
Accord	Silver	400
Accord	Black	500

"Origin" table

Model	Color	Origin
Camaro	Yellow	Canada
Camaro	Black	United States
Camaro	Red	United States
Corolla	Black	Canada
Corolla	Silver	Mexico
Corolla	Gold	Canada
Corolla	White	Mexico
Mustang	Black	United States
Mustang	Silver	United States
Focus	Silver	Mexico
Focus	Black	Canada
Focus	Burgundy	Canada
Accord	Silver	Mexico
Accord	Black	United States

"Year" table

Model	Color	Year_Produced
Camaro	Yellow	2021
Camaro	Black	2020
Camaro	Red	2022
Corolla	Black	2019
Corolla	Silver	2020
Corolla	Gold	2021
Corolla	White	2021
Mustang	Black	2019
Mustang	Silver	2019
Focus	Silver	2022
Focus	Black	2019
Focus	Burgundy	2022
Accord	Silver	2021
Accord	Black	2022

Questions

1. Create a view named "CarDetails" that combines model, color, origin, and production year for cars produced in 2022.
2. Create a list of all unique models sold or produced in 2019.
3. Find the total number of cars sold for each model in 2021.
4. Calculate the average number of units produced in 2020 for each model.
5. List models that sold more than 200 units in 2021.
6. Show the models and colors of cars that were sold, including those not produced.
7. Find the models and colors of cars that were produced but not sold.

8. List all models and their production years, including those with no sales data.
9. Retrieve the models, colors, and origins of cars sold in 2021.
10. Combine sales and production data for all models and colors.

Answer Key

1.

```
-- Create the view
CREATE VIEW CarDetails AS
SELECT m.Model, m.Color, o.Origin,
y.Year_Produced
FROM Model m
JOIN Origin o ON m.Model = o.Model AND
m.Color = o.Color
JOIN Year y ON m.Model = y.Model AND
m.Color = y.Color
WHERE y.Year_Produced = 2022;


-- Alter the view (change the year)
CREATE VIEW CarDetails AS
SELECT m.Model, m.Color, o.Origin,
y.Year_Produced
FROM Model m
JOIN Origin o ON m.Model = o.Model AND
m.Color = o.Color
JOIN Year y ON m.Model = y.Model AND
m.Color = y.Color
WHERE y.Year_Produced = 2021;
```

```
-- Drop the view
DROP VIEW CarDetails;
```

2.

```
-- Using UNION (to eliminate duplicates)
SELECT DISTINCT Model
FROM (
    SELECT Model FROM Model WHERE Model IN
(SELECT Model FROM Year WHERE
Year_Produced = 2019)
    UNION
    SELECT Model FROM Produced WHERE Model
IN (SELECT Model FROM Year WHERE
Year_Produced = 2019)
) AS UniqueModels;
```

3.

```
SELECT m.Model, SUM(m.Units_Sold) AS
Total_Sold
FROM Model m
JOIN Year y ON m.Model = y.Model AND
m.Color = y.Color
WHERE y.Year_Produced = 2021
GROUP BY m.Model;
```

4.

```
SELECT p.Model, AVG(p.Units_Produced) AS
Avg_Produced
FROM Produced p
```

```
JOIN Year y ON p.Model = y.Model AND
p.Color = y.Color
WHERE y.Year_Produced = 2020
GROUP BY p.Model;
```

5.

```
SELECT m.Model
FROM Model m
JOIN Year y ON m.Model = y.Model AND
m.Color = y.Color
WHERE y.Year_Produced = 2021 AND m.Units_-
Sold > 200;
```

6.

```
SELECT Model, Color FROM Model
UNION
SELECT Model, Color FROM Produced;
```

7.

```
SELECT p.Model, p.Color
FROM Produced p
LEFT JOIN Model m ON p.Model = m.Model AND
p.Color = m.Color
WHERE m.Units_Sold IS NULL;
```

8.

```
SELECT m.Model, y.Year_Produced
FROM Model m
```

```
FULL JOIN Year y ON m.Model = y.Model AND
m.Color = y.Color;
```

9.

```
SELECT m.Model, m.Color, o.Origin
FROM Model m
JOIN Origin o ON m.Model = o.Model AND
m.Color = o.Color
JOIN Year y ON m.Model = y.Model AND
m.Color = y.Color
WHERE y.Year_Produced = 2021;
```

10.

```
SELECT m.Model, m.Color, COALESCE(m.Unit-
s_Sold, 0) AS Units_Sold, COALESCE(p.Unit-
s_Produced, 0) AS Units_Produced
FROM Model m
LEFT JOIN Produced p ON m.Model = p.Model
AND m.Color = p.Color;
```

How did you do with these exercises? I can bet that you did really well! Good job! Now that you have mastered the intermediate skills for querying in SQL, it is time to take the last step and move on to the most challenging use of the language. As you move on to the next chapter, you are going to learn useful advanced techniques to apply to your database using SQL and finally master its use.

Chapter 6
Advanced SQL
Techniques

In the previous chapters, we have seen the basic and intermediate uses of SQL in databases. However, when you are dealing with RDBMS that contains too many tables, repeated information, or needs a more complex analysis of the data, some of the techniques you have previously seen might not be enough. For this reason, in this last chapter of SQL techniques, I want to provide you with some of the advanced features of SQL that can be applied to carry out analyses that require more processing or even dealing with exceptions.

You will see that with the advanced techniques and concepts taught in this chapter, you will be able to build complex projects to showcase your abilities in your portfolio. Once you are done reading and learning the concepts taught here, you will master manipulating and analyzing data using SQL, which will be reinforced with the exercises in this chapter.

If you are ready to embark on this last part of the book before starting to build your own project, join me in learning some concepts that will help take you to the next level as a data analyst and help propel you in your career.

Advanced SQL Techniques

To learn more about the advanced techniques in this section, you will notice that there are a few more tables than you have seen in the previous parts of this book. While these are just examples created using fictional data, when you are working on your own project it will help you have an idea of what should be collected to ensure that your capabilities are shown to their utmost potential. Here are the tables you will need to use for these exercises. (Please note that additional tables will be provided on some of the exercises for optimal comprehension).

Employee information table

Employee ID	FirstName	LastName	Email	StartDate
101	Gary	Oleman	gary.oleman@email.com	2021-01-15
102	Sarah	Pierce	sarah.pierce@email.com	2020-03-10
103	Judy	Bush	judy.bush@email.com	2019-12-05
104	James	Anderson	james.anderson@email.com	2022-05-20
105	Michael	Davis	michael.d@email.com	2021-09-08

Project information table

ProjectID	ProjectName	Manager	EmployeesCount
101	Project X	Gary Oleman	3
102	Project Y	Sarah Pierce	2
103	Project Z	Judy Bush	2
104	Project A	James Anderson	4
105	Project B	Michael Davis	3

Customer information table

CustomerID	FirstName	LastName	Email	OrderCount
301	Lisa	Brown	lisa.brown@email.com	2
302	Michael	Wilson	michael.w@email.com	3
303	Karen	Lee	karen.lee@email.com	1
304	Richard	Lewis	richard.l@email.com	2
305	Emily	Hall	emily.h@email.com	4

Order information table

OrderID	CustomerName	ProductName	TotalAmount
401	Lisa Brown	Laptop	899.99
402	Lisa Brown	Smartphone	599.99
403	Michael Wilson	Tablet	449.99
404	Karen Lee	Headphones	79.99
405	Richard Lewis	Laptop	899.99
406	Emily Hall	Monitor	349.99
407	Lisa Brown	Speaker	129.99

Product information table

ProductID	ProductName	Category	Supplier	UnitsSold
501	Laptop	Electronics	Supplier A	1000
502	Smartphone	Electronics	Supplier B	800
503	Tablet	Electronics	Supplier C	600
504	Headphones	Electronics	Supplier D	1200
505	Monitor	Electronics	Supplier A	300
506	Speaker	Electronics	Supplier C	500

Employees' skills table

EmployeeID	FirstName	LastName	SkillName	ProficiencyLevel
101	Gary	Oleman	SQL	2
101	Gary	Oleman	Java	2
102	Sarah	Pierce	SQL	3
102	Sarah	Pierce	Python	2
103	Judy	Bush	SQL	2
103	Judy	Bush	JavaScript	1
104	James	Anderson	Data Analysis	3
105	Michael	Davis	Python	4

Sales history table

Sale ID	Product Name	Customer Name	Sale Date	Quantity	Total Amount
701	Laptop	Lisa Brown	2023-04-03	2	1799.98
702	Smartphone	Michael Wilson	2023-04-03	3	1799.97
703	Tablet	Karen Lee	2023-04-03	1	449.99
704	Monitor	Richard Lewis	2023-04-03	4	1399.96

Common table expressions (CTEs): These are tables that enable the user to carry out complex queries without the need to create complex SQL structures or subqueries in the code. One of the great advantages of these tables is that it makes grouping data and carrying out calculations easier, as well as joining information that is contained in different tables. Shin (2022) compares these temporary tables to writing essays, in which you are going to break the content into paragraphs so the information is easier to understand.

- **Syntax:**

```
WITH cte_name (column1, column2, ...) AS (
SELECT column1, column2, ...
FROM table_name
WHERE condition -- Optional filter
GROUP BY -- Optional GROUP BY clause
HAVING-- Optional HAVING clause
ORDER BY -- Optional ORDER BY clause
)
SELECT column1, column2, ...
FROM cte_name;
```

- **Example:** Using the "Salaries" table, create a CTE to filter employees with salaries above $50,000.

```
WITH HighSalaryEmployees AS (
SELECT FirstName, LastName
FROM Salaries
WHERE Salary > 50000
)
SELECT * FROM HighSalaryEmployees;
```

Recursive CTEs: This resource uses CTEs but, instead of referencing another table, it references itself. This means it can be used to create a hierarchy structure, for example, between employees and managers, with the data contained within a table. Here, the key is to use the "UNION ALL" feature to reference it to the original table from which you are extracting the data.

- **Syntax:**

```
WITH RecursiveCTE AS (
SELECT column1, column2, …
FROM table_name
WHERE condition -- Optional filter
UNION ALL
SELECT column1, column2, …
FROM table_name
WHERE related_condition -- Optional filter
)
SELECT column1, column2, …
FROM RecursiveCTE;
```

- **Example:** Suppose that you have the database table, and you want to create an organogram to show the hierarchy structure of the company. By using the table "employees," create a self-referencing relationship that will represent the information.

```
WITH RecursiveCTE AS (
SELECT employee_id, first_name, last_name,
manager_id
FROM Employees
WHERE manager_id IS NULL
UNION ALL
SELECT E.employee_id, E.first_name,
E.last_name, E.manager_id
FROM Employees E
INNER JOIN RecursiveCTE R
ON E.manager_id = R.employee_id
)
```

```
SELECT employee_id, first_name, last_name,
manager_id
FROM
RecursiveCTE;
```

Join CTE: In this case, you are once again using CTEs, but using the "JOIN" feature to associate different tables within the database. This can be used when you want to join columns from different tables to create another table without building complex subqueries to the code.

- **Syntax:**

```
WITH JoinCTE AS (
SELECT column1, column2,
--Replace with the name of your first
table or subquery
FROM table1
--Replace with the name of your second
table or subquery
INNER JOIN table2
--Replace with the join condition that
connects the tables
ON table1.column_name = table2.column_nam
)
-- Additional SELECT statements and joins
if needed
--Replace with the columns you want to
select in your final result set
SELECT column1, column2,
--Reference the Join CTE you defined
earlier
FROM
```

```
JoinCTE;
```

- **Example:** Now, we want to create a Join CTE to retrieve information about employees, their salaries, and positions using the employees, salaries, and positions table.

```
WITH JoinCTE AS (
SELECT E.first_name, E.last_name,
S.salary, P.position
FROM Employees E
INNER JOIN Salaries S
ON E.employee_id = S.employee_id
INNER JOIN Positions P
ON E.employee_id = P.employee_id
)
SELECT first_name, last_name, salary,
position
FROM
JoinCTE;
```

Creating roles: While this feature is relatively easy, not all users know how to apply it. When you create a role within an RDBMS using SQL, you are assigning privileges to a certain group or person to access a part of this database. You will use this feature to maintain the structure and security of the original table by determining if the access will be granted by using "CONNECT," "RESOURCE," and, "DBA," depending on the permission you want the person or group to have. This is a more sophisticated alternative to granting or revoking privileges in a database that can become a complex process when there are too many users accessing the same data.

- **Syntax:**

```
CREATE ROLE role_name;
GRANT privilege_name TO role_name;
```

- **Example:** Suppose you want to create a role to have access to "HR" and grant them permission to access employee data. The code should create an "HR" role and grant it permission to select data from the "Employees" table.

```
CREATE ROLE HR;
GRANT SELECT ON Employees TO HR;
```

Triggers: The function of a trigger can be defined as establishing that a certain action should be carried out when an event happens in the database. These triggers could be applied in several different instances, such as updating the date and time or the name and department of an employee if there is a change in a connected table within the database. These triggers are automatic, which means that they cannot be carried out manually. However, much like updating the date of a database to "today" so it matches the date of when you open it, these transactions cannot be rolled back or canceled after a trigger has been invoked.

- **Syntax:**

```
CREATE TRIGGER trigger_name
ON table_name
FOR [INSERT, UPDATE, DELETE]
AS
BEGIN
-- Enter trigger logic here
END;
```

- **Example:** Suppose you want to create a trigger in the employee information table. This trigger should automatically update the "LastModified" timestamp whenever a record in the table is updated.

```
CREATE TRIGGER UpdateTimestamp
ON EmployeeInformation
FOR UPDATE
AS
BEGIN
UPDATE EmployeeInformation
SET LastModified = GETDATE()
WHERE EmployeeID IN (SELECT EmployeeID
FROM inserted);
END;
```

Transaction layers: When you establish a transaction layer in a database, this means that you will write a code that will carry out a specific task. This, or these, tasks, when happening, will have two results: The first is that the database will become unavailable while it is being carried out, and the second is that with the "COMMIT" command, once the transaction is finished, the database will be available again. It is important to note that, as we have seen previously, this command of applying transaction layers will ensure that the database maintains its ACID characteristics.

- **Syntax:**

```
BEGIN TRANSACTION;
-- Insert here the SQL statements within
the transaction
COMMIT;
```

- **Example:** Suppose you have a database that stores employee information, and you need to perform two operations atomically: updating an employee's salary in the "Salaries" table and recording the transaction in the "TransactionLog" table.

```
BEGIN TRANSACTION;
-- Step 1: Update the employee's salary in
the "Salaries" table
UPDATE Salaries
SET Salary = 60000
WHERE FirstName = 'Gary' AND LastName =
'Oleman';
-- Step 2: Insert a log entry in the
"TransactionLog" table
INSERT INTO TransactionLog (EmployeeID,
TransactionType, TransactionDate)
VALUES ( (SELECT EmployeeID FROM Employees
WHERE FirstName = 'Gary' AND LastName =
'Oleman'), 'Salary Update',
GETDATE() );
-- If any step fails, the entire transac-
tion will be rolled back
COMMIT;
```

Distributed transactions: Similarly to a transaction you have just read about, when you carry out distributed transactions you are going to have the action be carried out among two or more different databases. While in the previous example, the situation will be applied within one RDBMS, in this case, you are "distributing" the action among other databases. In the final part of the code, you will notice that it is able to "COMMIT" the changes if there is no error or the possibility to "ROLLBACK" if any errors are identified.

Syntax:

```
-- Begin distributed transaction
BEGIN DISTRIBUTED TRANSACTION;
-- SQL statements for distributed
operations
-- Commit or Rollback the distributed
transaction
COMMIT DISTRIBUTED TRANSACTION;
-- or ROLLBACK DISTRIBUTED TRANSACTION;
```

- **Example:** For this example, you are not going to use the tables provided because we are talking about different databases. Therefore, in this situation, we will use hypothetical databases ("Database A" and "Database B") to illustrate what the syntax will be. The idea here is to transfer the data between them in a distributed transaction.

```
BEGIN DISTRIBUTED TRANSACTION;
INSERT INTO DatabaseA.dbo.TableA (column1,
column2)
VALUES ('Value1', 'Value2');
INSERT INTO DatabaseB.dbo.TableB (column3,
column4)
VALUES ('Value3', 'Value4');
COMMIT DISTRIBUTED TRANSACTION;
```

Temporary functions: As the name suggests, when you are carrying out a temporary function, you are asking the database to bring you a query result that will later be discarded and does not need to be stored. This makes the query that is being carried out simpler and easier to read since the code is cleaner, and can be broken down into parts.

- **Syntax:**

```
CREATE TEMPORARY FUNCTION
function_name (parameter1 data_type, para-
meter2 data_type)
RETURNS return_data_type
BEGIN
END;
```

- **Example:** Suppose you would like to know the average salary of a certain team or department, but that this information does not need to be stored.

```
CREATE TEMPORARY FUNCTION
CalculateAvgSalary(department_id INT)
RETURNS DECIMAL(10, 2)
BEGIN
DECLARE avg_salary DECIMAL(10, 2);
SELECT AVG(salary) INTO avg_salary
FROM Salaries
WHERE department_id = department_id;
RETURN avg_salary;
END;
```

Pivoting data using case when: According to Shin (2022), although "CASE WHEN" is a common function in SQL, few people know that this function can be used to pivot data in tables as well. This means that when you apply these statements, you will be able to divide the information and have a better visualization of the data if needed.

- **Syntax:**

```
SELECT column1, column2,
CASE
WHEN condition1 THEN result1
WHEN condition2 THEN result2
ELSE result3
END AS new_column
FROM table_name;
```

- **Example:** Suppose you want to rank the employees based on how much they earn. You will need to create a new table that will determine if their salary is within the ranges of low, medium, and high.

```
SELECT first_name, last_name, salary,
CASE
WHEN salary < 30000 THEN 'Low'
WHEN salary >= 30000 AND salary < 60000
THEN 'Medium'
ELSE 'High'
END AS salary_category
FROM Salaries;
```

Except versus not in: Many SQL developers confuse both of these concepts because they are so similar. While they are not wrong, since they both function in almost the same way, the main difference between using the "EXCEPT" code and the one for "NOT IN" is that in the first the duplicates will be filtered from the results, something that will not happen if you are using the latter. One important remark that should be made here is that when you use EXCEPT, the number of columns in the tables should be the same to enable comparing more than one column, in NOT IN, you will be able to compare only one column at a time.

- **Syntax (except):**

```
SELECT column1, column2
FROM table1
EXCEPT
SELECT column3, column4
FROM table2;
```

- **Syntax (not in):**SELECT column1, column2

```
FROM table1
WHERE (column1, column2) NOT IN (SELECT
column1, column2 FROM table2);
```

- **Example:** Suppose you want to carry out a query to find the information to regain employees who have not received any promotions by using tables "employees" and "promotions." Either query form could be used, although they would be structured differently.

```
-- Using EXCEPT
SELECT first_name, last_name
FROM employees
EXCEPT
SELECT first_name, last_name
FROM promotions;
```

```
-- Using NOT IN
SELECT first_name, last_name
FROM employees
WHERE (first_name, last_name) NOT IN
(SELECT first_name, last_name FROM
promotions);
```

Self joins: The concept of being able to join a table with itself, as the name expresses, might be confusing to some users. This is because it theoretically would not make sense to join information in a table with something it already contains. However, if you think about a table in which there are many columns and rows with data, this might be an alternative to having a better view of specific information it contains and is not immediately visible.

- **Syntax:**

```
SELECT t1.column_name, t2.column_name
FROM table_name t1
INNER JOIN table_name t2 ON t1.related_-
column = t2.related_column;
```

- **Example:** Use the "employees" table to find pairs of employees who share the same department.

```
SELECT e1.first_name, e1.last_name,
e2.first_name, e2.last_name
FROM Employees e1
INNER JOIN Employees e2 ON e1.department =
e2.department
WHERE e1.employee_id < e2.employee_id;
```

Row number and dense rank: One of the most common queries carried out in database tables is ranking information according to certain criteria. While the concept of "ranking" information is well understood, there are variations to it, such as assigning character-istics to a row and applying a dense rank to order the information. The difference between these is that while the dense rank does not contemplate duplicate information, when you apply the rank duplicates are considered, and in the row number they are assigned specific numbers according to the data used.

Syntax:

```
SELECT column1, column2,
RANK() OVER (PARTITION BY partition_column
ORDER BY order_column) AS rank_result,
DENSE_RANK() OVER (PARTITION BY parti-
tion_column ORDER BY order_column) AS
dense_rank_result,
ROW_NUMBER() OVER (PARTITION BY parti-
tion_column ORDER BY order_column) AS
row_number_result
FROM table_name;
```

- **Example:** Create an employee list by ranking them according to the salaries.

```
SELECT first_name, last_name, department,
salary,
RANK() OVER (PARTITION BY department ORDER
BY salary DESC) AS rank_result,
DENSE_RANK() OVER (PARTITION BY department
ORDER BY salary DESC) AS
dense_rank_result,
```

```
ROW_NUMBER() OVER (PARTITION BY department
ORDER BY salary DESC) AS row_number_result
FROM Employees;
```

Calculating delta values: This is a calculation code used for dealing usually with large numbers and identifying the delta variation between two or more data sources.

- **Syntax:**

```
SELECT column1, column2,
column_value - LAG(column_value) OVER
(ORDER BY order_column) AS delta
FROM table_name;
```

- **Example:** For this example, we are not going to use any of the previously seen tables. You are going to imagine that you want to analyze the change in the stock prices in a specific table (Stock Prices). The query should create a list of the stock process and changes that it has undergone, and reflect the values of the price change.

```
SELECT date, stock_price,
stock_price - LAG(stock_price) OVER (ORDER
BY date) AS price_change
FROM StockPrices;
```

Calculating running totals: As the name suggests, this function will bring you the cumulative results of a specific column by considering all the information it contains. For example, you can have a column with the monthly revenue of a company, and you will create a running total column for which these values will be added on a monthly basis to bring a total that considers the previous months as well.

- **Syntax:**

```
SELECT column1, column2,
SUM(column_value) OVER (ORDER BY order_-
column) AS running_total
FROM table_name;
```

- **Example:** Calculate what is the total revenue for a specific period from the "sales" table.

```
SELECT date, revenue,
SUM(revenue) OVER (ORDER BY date) AS cumu-
lative_revenue
FROM Sales;
```

Repeated and nested data: SQL has two advanced functions that allow users to join and separate data. When you use the "NESTED" function, you are going to aggregate the information from two different tables (in the same column or not), while there is also the UNNEST function, that will divide the information, for the cases in which you have more than one information in a column. At the same time, with the repeated function, you will be able to duplicate information to one or more columns that need to have the same information.

- **Syntax:**

```
SELECT column1, column2,
FROM
`project_id.dataset_id._table_id`,
UNNEST(your_nested_field) AS unnested_-
field_alias
WHERE condition1 AND condition2
ORDER BY column1, column2,
LIMIT limit_value;
```

- **Example:** Suppose the employee skills table was structured as below, and you wanted to create a table in which the separate skills would be divided each into a different row.

EmployeeID	FirstName	LastName	Skills
101	Gary	Oleman	["SQL", "Java"]
102	Sarah	Pierce	["SQL", "Python"]
103	Judy	Bush	["SQL", "JavaScript"]
104	James	Anderson	["Data Analysis"]
105	Michael	Davis	["Python"]

```
SELECT EmployeeID, SkillName
FROM
`your_project.your_dataset.employ-
ee_skills`, UNNEST(Skills) AS SkillName
WHERE condition1
ORDER BY EmployeeID, SkillName
LIMIT limit_value;
```

String functions: These are advanced SQL queries that can be used to manage data with STRING content. Here, there is no specific syntax to be applied because it will depend on which technique you are going to apply. These can include features such as "LOWER," "CONCAT," and others. You can apply these to one or more tables, columns, and databases. As a refresher, here is a list of some string functions that can be applied to SQL:

Function Name	Description	Syntax
LOWER()	It converts a string to lowercase letters.	SELECT LOWER(column_name) FROM table_name;
UPPER()	Is used to convert a string to uppercase letters.	SELECT UPPER(column_name) FROM table_name;
CONCAT()	Is used to concatenate two or more strings.	SELECT CONCAT(first_name, ' ', last_name) AS full_name FROM employees;
LENGTH()	Is used to return the length (number of characters) of a string.	SELECT LENGTH(column_name) FROM table_name;
SUBSTRING( )	Is used to extract a part of a string based on a specified position and length.	SELECT SUBSTRING(column_name, start_position, length) FROM table_name;
TRIM()	Is used to remove leading and trailing spaces from a string.	SELECT TRIM(column_name) FROM table_name;
LEFT()	Is used to return the leftmost characters of a string.	SELECT LEFT(column_name, n) FROM table_name;
RIGHT()	Is used to return the rightmost characters of a string.	SELECT RIGHT(column_name, n) FROM table_name;

- **Example:** To generate a report, unite the first and last names of the employees that are in different columns to create a list with their full names.

```
SELECT CONCAT(first_name, ' ', last_name)
AS full_name
FROM Employees;
```

Subqueries: Similarly to the string functions, these will depend on the subqueries you want to carry out and the items you want to find. A subquery is a query that is carried out with a query. While they are constantly used to make the database bring back the information you need, having too many of these might make the processing time slower and the query less efficient. It will also make the code harder to read and, thus, should be applied with caution. To carry out a subquery, you can use the different statements and functions listed below:

Name	Description	Example Usage
AVG()	Is used to calculate the average value of a numeric column.	SELECT AVG(column_name) FROM table_name;
SUM()	Is used to calculate the sum of values in a numeric column.	SELECT SUM(column_name) FROM table_name;
COUNT()	Is used to count the number of rows or non-null values in a column.	SELECT COUNT(column_name) FROM table_name;
MIN()	Is used to return the minimum value in a column.	SELECT MIN(column_name) FROM table_name;
MAX()	Is used to return the maximum value in a column.	SELECT MAX(column_name) FROM table_name;
EXISTS()	Is used to check for the existence of rows in a subquery result.	SELECT column_name FROM table_name WHERE EXISTS (SELECT * FROM subquery_table);
IN()	Is used to test if a value matches any value in a subquery result.	SELECT column_name FROM table_name WHERE column_name IN (SELECT subquery_column FROM subquery_table);
ANY()	Is used to compare a value to any value in a subquery result.	SELECT column_name FROM table_name WHERE column_name < ANY (SELECT subquery_column FROM subquery_table);
ALL()	Is used to compare a value to all values in a subquery result.	SELECT column_name FROM table_name WHERE column_name > ALL (SELECT subquery_column FROM subquery_table);

- **Example:** Use the tables given as an example to find the average salary of all the IT team members.

```
SELECT department, AVG(salary) AS
avg_salary
FROM Employees
WHERE department = 'IT';
```

Date time functions: As the name suggests, date time functions will be applied to carry out queries that involve data within the database that have these characteristics. Much like the previous functions we have seen there is no specific syntax that can be used. It will depend on the type of information you want to express and if they are composed of time, date, and time or date. Can be used with different statements and functions, including:

Function Name	Description	Example Usage
GETDATE()	Returns the current date and time.	SELECT GETDATE();
DATEADD()	Adds or subtracts a specified time interval to a date.	SELECT DATEADD(day, 7, date_column) FROM table_name;
DATEDIFF()	Calculates the difference between two dates or times.	SELECT DATEDIFF(day, date1, date2) FROM table_name;
DATEPART()	Returns a specific part of a date or time, such as the year or month.	SELECT DATEPART(year, date_column) FROM table_name;
YEAR(), MONTH(), DAY()	Returns the year, month, or date of a date.	SELECT YEAR / MONTH / DAY (date_column) FROM table_name;
HOUR(), MINUTE(), SECOND()	Returns the hour, minute or second of a time.	SELECT HOUR / MINUTE / SECOND (time_column) FROM table_name;
CONVERT()	Converts one data type to another, including date formats.	SELECT CONVERT(varchar, date_column, 106) FROM table_name;
FORMAT()	Formats a date or time according to a specified format.	SELECT FORMAT(date_column, 'yyyy-MM-dd') FROM table_name;
SYSDATETIME()	Returns the current date and time with high precision.	SELECT SYSDATETIME();
DATEFROMPARTS()	Constructs a date from year, month, and day parts.	SELECT DATEFROMPARTS(2023, 9, 15);

- **Example:** Use the employees' table to calculate the age of all the company's employees.

```
SELECT first_name, last_name, birthdate,
DATEDIFF(YEAR, birthdate, GETDATE())
AS age
FROM Employees;
```

Since in this chapter we have talked about advanced SQL queries, one of the topics that should be mentioned before you start the exercises and build your own project is the *performance* of the analysis you will carry out. Performance is an essential component of dealing with SQL databases because it can significantly impact the time and quality of the information you are going to receive. Therefore, in the next section, you are going to learn some tips and tricks to enhance the database and query performance.

Optimizing Performance

When you are dealing with a database, it is always important to take into consideration the size of the tables you are going to apply the query to and what you are going to select for the analysis to take place. Several factors impact the database performance and can lead to slower processing times and more difficulty in obtaining the information you want within an adequate time. Here are the most common factors that affect database performance:

- The database has too many tables.
- The size of the table you are using (if it contains too much data, for example).
- Hardware limitations.
- Software updates.
- Running multiple queries at the same time.

- Multiple users running queries simultaneously.
- Using too many subqueries and aggregations.
- Complex querying that requires more processing rather than using simple code.
- Lack of indexes.
- Having too many "join" commands in a table.
- Using too many or too complicated "join" commands at a time.
- Selecting too much information to carry out the query (such as using SELECT * when you only want to access a few columns).

If you want to ensure that you have optimal performance and that the queries are as efficient as possible, here are some items you should consider when writing code or managing tables:

- Select for the query only the data you are going to use (the specific columns and items you want it to consider).
- Reduce the size of the table(s) or optimize their information structure.
- Monitor performance by using the code show_time_to_run() to identify how long it will take a query to run.
- Avoid using subqueries with too many statements or conditions.
- Ensure that all the data in the table has the correct data type.
- Invest in database design to ensure that the structure that it will be built with will provide optimal processing times.
- Establish a plan to run the queries if you are using more than one.
- Divide the processing into smaller sets of data to make the processing more efficient.

By using these techniques when managing the database for queries, it is likely that you will achieve a better processing time. You should remember that the more statements your code has, the more complicated it will be, and it is likely that the query will take more time to process. If you apply these simple best practices to your code, you will certainly achieve the results you desire.

Exercises

Tables

Destinations

Destination ID	Destination Name	Country	Region	Average Temperature	Travel Cost
1	Paris	France	Europe	22	1500
2	New York	USA	North America	28	2000
3	Tokyo	Japan	Asia	30	2500
4	Sydney	Australia	Australia	25	3000
5	Cancun	Mexico	North America	32	1800
6	Rome	Italy	Europe	27	1600
7	Dubai	UAE	Middle East	35	2800
8	Rio de Janeiro	Brazil	South America	31	2200
9	Cape Town	South Africa	Africa	26	2700
10	Bangkok	Thailand	Asia	33	2100

Clients

ClientID	FirstName	LastName	Email	Phone
101	Maria	Rodriguez	maria@email.com	+1234567890
102	Michael	Smith	michael@email.com	+1987654321
103	Sofia	Lee	sofia@email.com	+3456789012
104	Ahmed	Khan	ahmed@email.com	+5678901234
105	Elena	Petrov	elena@email.com	+6789012345
106	Diego	Fernandez	diego@email.com	+7890123456

Flights

FlightID	DestinationID	DepartureDate	ReturnDate	Price
501	1	2023-07-10	2023-07-20	800
502	2	2023-08-15	2023-08-25	900
503	3	2023-09-05	2023-09-15	950
504	4	2023-07-20	2023-07-30	1100
505	5	2023-08-30	2023-09-09	850
506	6	2023-09-10	2023-09-20	750

Employees

EmployeeID	FirstName	LastName	Position	Salary
201	Emily	Anderson	Sales Representative	50000
202	David	Martinez	Travel Consultant	55000
203	Sophia	Nguyen	Marketing Manager	60000
204	Daniel	Wilson	Operations Manager	65000
205	Emma	Garcia	Finance Manager	70000
206	Ethan	Davis	IT Specialist	55000

Bookings

BookingID	ClientID	FlightID	BookingDate	Status
301	101	501	2023-06-20	Confirmed
302	101	502	2023-07-05	Confirmed
303	102	501	2023-06-22	Confirmed
304	103	503	2023-07-15	Pending
305	104	504	2023-07-30	Confirmed
306	105	505	2023-08-10	Pending

Questions

1. Create a new database role named "TravelAgents" and grant SELECT privileges on the "Clients" and "Flights" tables to this role.
2. Create a trigger that automatically updates the "BookingDate" to the current date when a new booking is added to the "Bookings" table.
3. Set in place a transaction layer that inserts a new client into the "Clients" table and a corresponding booking into the "Bookings" table. Ensure that both insertions are successful or rolled back together.
4. Implement a distributed transaction that updates the "Salary" of an employee in the "Employees" table and deducts the corresponding amount from the "TotalAmount" in the 'Bookings' table for the same client.
5. Write a query using CTE to retrieve the client names and the number of bookings they have made.
6. Write a query to pivot data that displays the total number of bookings for each status ("Confirmed" and "Pending") separately.
7. Find clients who have not made bookings using both the EXCEPT and NOT IN operators.

8. Calculate the running total of the "TotalAmount" in the "Bookings" table for each client, ordered by booking date.

9. Write a query to retrieve the names of clients who have booked flights, along with the destination names of those flights.

10. Create a list of clients with email addresses starting with "michael."

11. Find the clients who have made the highest number of bookings.

12. Obtain a list of flights that will depart after September 1, 2023, and display the mentioned dates in a human-readable format.

Answer Key

1.

```
CREATE ROLE TravelAgents;
GRANT SELECT ON Clients TO TravelAgents;
GRANT SELECT ON Flights TO TravelAgents;
```

2.

```
CREATE TRIGGER update_booking_date_trigger
BEFORE INSERT ON Bookings
FOR EACH ROW
BEGIN
SET NEW.BookingDate = CURRENT_DATE;
END;
```

3.

```
BEGIN;
SAVEPOINT savepoint1;
INSERT INTO Clients (FirstName, LastName,
Email, Phone)
VALUES ('Sophie, 'Lake',
'sophie.lake@email.com', '+1234567890');
INSERT INTO Bookings (ClientID, FlightID,
BookingDate, Status)
VALUES (currval(pg_get_serial_se-
quence('Clients', 'ClientID')), 501,
CURRENT_DATE, 'Confirmed');
COMMIT;
```

4.

```
BEGIN;
UPDATE Employees
SET Salary = Salary + 5000
WHERE EmployeeID = 201;
UPDATE Bookings
SET Status = 'Confirmed'
WHERE BookingID = 301;
COMMIT;
```

5.

```
WITH ClientBookings AS (
SELECT c.FirstName, c.LastName,
COUNT(b.BookingID) AS BookingCount
FROM Clients c
```

```
LEFT JOIN Bookings b ON c.ClientID =
b.ClientID
GROUP BY c.FirstName, c.LastName
)
SELECT * FROM ClientBookings;
```

6.

```
SELECT
COUNT(CASE WHEN Status = 'Confirmed' THEN
1 ELSE NULL END) AS ConfirmedCount,
COUNT(CASE WHEN Status = 'Pending' THEN 1
ELSE NULL END) AS PendingCount
FROM Bookings;
```

7.

```
— Using EXCEPT
SELECT FirstName, LastName
FROM Clients
EXCEPT
SELECT c.FirstName, c.LastName
FROM Clients c
JOIN Bookings b ON c.ClientID = b.Clien-
tID;ç

-- Using NOT IN
SELECT FirstName, LastName
FROM
```

8.

```
SELECT ClientID, BookingDate,
SUM(TotalAmount) OVER (PARTITION BY
ClientID ORDER BY BookingDate) AS
RunningTotal
FROM Bookings
ORDER BY ClientID, BookingDate;
```

9.

```
SELECT FirstName || ' ' || LastName AS
ClientName,
ARRAY_AGG(
STRUCT(
DestinationName AS DestinationName,
DepartureDate AS DepartureDate,
ReturnDate AS ReturnDate
)
) AS BookedDestinations
FROM Clients
LEFT JOIN Bookings ON Clients.ClientID =
Bookings.ClientID
LEFT JOIN Flights ON Bookings.FlightID =
Flights.FlightID
WHERE Bookings.ClientID IS NOT NULL
GROUP BY Clients.ClientID,
Clients.FirstName, Clients.LastName;
```

10.

```
SELECT FirstName, LastName, Email
FROM Clients
WHERE LOWER(Email) LIKE 'michael%';
```

11.

```
SELECT FirstName, LastName, Email
FROM Clients
WHERE ClientID = (
SELECT ClientID
FROM Bookings
GROUP BY ClientID
ORDER BY COUNT(*) DESC
LIMIT 1
);
```

12.

```
SELECT FlightID, DestinationID,
TO_DATE(DepartureDate) AS DepartureDate
FROM Flights
WHERE DepartureDate > '2023-09-01';
```

How did you do? Remember that you should use this book as a guide, and it should help you identify potential examples in case you want to practice any additional queries. Continuously testing your skills and working on different techniques to manage data will be an incredible asset, especially when you need to answer interview questions. You can create your own questions and business problems to determine what the skills you would like to focus on are and even look online for potential examples. As a matter of fact, you should know that if you do not yet have the hardware capacity to download all the data and programs you will need, there are several websites that can help you practice online. These include LeetCode, Hacker Rank, DataLemur, SQLZoo, and SQLPad for practicing interview questions for SQL.

Chapter 7
Putting It All Together

Are you excited to start putting together your one project? I can bet you are! You have learned so far the most important SQL techniques, and they will give you the ability and skills to start building your own projects and manage databases you might have to deal with at work. If your goal is to use the knowledge you have acquired to change professions, then you are also on a great path to do so.

In this chapter, you are going to see some of the areas and industries that might require this knowledge and how it can be applied. In addition to this, you will also learn more about the profession of a data analyst. If you are ready to uncover the final details about this profession and start building your own project, join me in reading the last chapter of this book that will prepare you for the market.

Finding Your Niche

All of the techniques you have seen so far can be used by a professional interested in data analytics. According to Simplilearn (2023b), "the process of cleaning, analyzing, interpreting, and displaying data using different approaches and business intelligence tools is known as data analysis. Data analysis tools assist you in uncovering key insights that lead to better informed and successful decision-making." This data will be used and transformed into visual material, explanations, and statistics that can be interpreted by a company's shareholders to aid in the decision-making process.

However, a data analyst does more than just managing and querying the database or inputting information into it. They are also responsible for their maintenance, organization, correcting incorrect data, and ensuring that the results are trustworthy for patterns, predictions, and trends to be discovered. The data analyst will also be in charge of ensuring that the query code is correct to obtain the desired result and to grant or restrict permission to other people or groups.

The analysis can vary according to the purpose for which it will be used. They could, for example, make a statistical analysis to understand the reasons for a certain problem or perform a predictive analysis to identify trends. Other types of analysis include transforming text into usable data in a database, called text analysis, run diagnostics on why a certain event is happening and its causes in the diagnostic analysis, or even help a company's management decide the best course of action by performing a prescriptive analysis.

One of the ways to determine in which field you would like to work is to build some projects of your own. By practicing with the data sets available in repositories and in several online sources, you will be able to look into the different manners of managing data and identifying the one that fits your interests the best. Additionally, working on these projects will help you build a steady portfolio to showcase your skills and abilities with SQL. Many companies ask for this information to analyze the candidate and how they put their rationale into action.

Why Do You Need a Portfolio?

While you might be new to data analytics and, therefore, you have no specific work experience to account for, this does not mean that you cannot create a portfolio. In fact, it is so common to have professionals create and work on personal projects on their own time that there are platforms that host these publicly for anyone who wants to see your work. The two main places to have your project posted and attract the attention of potential recruiters in the market are Kaggle and GitHub.

Both of these websites have an incredibly large community that will give you visibility and help you in case you need troubleshooting for a specific subject. In addition to this, you should not forget the ability of social media. In this case, the specific reference is LinkedIn, where you will be able not to only post a link to your online projects, but also post presentations, images, and other results of the data analysis project you are working on.

The most important part of your portfolio is certainly the code and the skills you demonstrate, but there are also a few details that should not be forgotten. These skills include not only the code you are using to query the database, but also your ability to clean the data, obtain data from online sources, identify a clear problem you are trying to solve, the way you communicate the results, and the tools you are using to carry out all these processes. To demonstrate these abilities, remember that most resources are acceptable: video, screenshots, demonstrations, step-by-step guides, and other solutions you might think are appropriate.

You must remember that the more information you have on the project, the more details the recruiter will have on your skills. This means you should focus on the project and the code rather than your previous work experiences if they are not relevant or too much detail on your personal information. One of the great things about the internet is that you can look at other developers' portfolios and information to see what they did and didn't do to guide you on developing yours.

Of course, it should also be mentioned that you should only include projects that show the best of your abilities. If you are unsure about posting something, you can ask someone from the community to take a look and give their opinion on what needs work and what can be improved. If you are just starting to build your portfolio, remember to look into subjects that interest you. This way, you will be motivated to carry out the analysis and the passion will be conveyed to those looking at the project.

Determining the topic of your first project and the ones to come is not as difficult as it seems. You might find out that it is more difficult to find quality and reliable data than the analysis itself. For this reason, it is important that you look into the raw data before starting and identify if it contains all the information you need to answer the question you are working on. After this is done, all you will need to do is prepare the data, so you can start querying. Some ideas you can explore for this purpose include analyzing:

- statistics for your favorite sports team
- metrics on social media for your favorite band
- information on books you have read and their details

- sales and revenue data for a specific company or market
- numbers and trends for the stock market
- information regarding the students in your class
- government-released data

There are several data set sources on the internet that you can choose from, varying from official websites (government, police, etc.) to fictional databases provided by platforms such as Kaggle, which are used just for showcasing skills. Another good source to obtain this information are the online repositories that provide the data without cost for users who are learning and practicing. You can also create your own data set by creating a table with data from different sources.

Regardless of the data set you are going to use or the business problem you are going to solve, the essential matter is to put to use code that will show you can manage simple, intermediate, and advanced SQL techniques. This being said, let's move on to the exciting part, in which you are going to learn how to build your own project!

Crafting Your Portfolio Project

Although GitHub and Kaggle were previously mentioned as platforms to host your portfolio, there are several others that can also be used for this purpose. These include Maven Analytics, Slideshare LeetCode, Mode, and DataCamp Workspace. Determining the best one for your projects will depend on the job you are pursuing and the focus you want to give it. One of the best ways to determine if the online platform is the best for you is to scroll through some projects and see what is being posted and the language being used as well as the data set availability for uses if it is paid, and what the advantages it presents are.

Creating Your Project in Kaggle

For this project example, I am going to use Kaggle and provide you with the step-by-step process of starting your project. Are you ready?

The first thing you will need to do is identify the subject of the project you are going to work on. Although not crucial since you are just starting to use and get familiarized with SQL, you should establish the dialect you want to use, as this will make a difference when establishing the data types. Next, you need to identify the question you are going to answer, the information you need to carry out this analysis, and what is the objective of the project. Essentially speaking, you want to answer the questions: *What question am I trying to answer?* or, *What problem am I trying to solve?*

Once you have done this, you need to find a data set that can be applied to the project and analyzed accordingly. In Kaggle, under the "datasets" tab, you will find several different options to choose from. They are all separated by themes and applications, including those for computer science and education divided into sports, health, finance, and data on social issues. You can use the search bar to find more information.

Next, you will establish the metrics and goals you are trying to achieve and what is the data you need to find to do this. You will then collect and clean the data before starting to work with it. Once this is done, all that is left is to analyze it, reach the conclusions that will answer your questions, and place the results in a visual manner that will be understandable to those looking at it.

Here is a quick overview of the process:

- **Step 1:** Define your goals and the question you need to answer.
- **Step 2:** Determine how to measure set goals.
- **Step 3:** Collect your data.
- **Step 4:** Clean the data.
- **Step 5:** Analyze your data by using the SQL techniques you have learned.
- **Step 6:** Interpret results and draw conclusions.

This process will usually be the standard applied to most of the matters that require a data analysis process. There will eventually be some differences according to the database used and the source for the collected data. However, if you follow the process that has been shown herein, you will certainly achieve the results you are looking for.

Spread the Word

This is your chance to let others know that SQL is, indeed, just another language. With the help of this guide, they can further their careers as developers, data managers—or any profession in which handling and retrieving data is the norm.

Simply by sharing your honest opinion of this book and what you've learned, you'll show new readers where they can find a comprehensive guide to SQL—starting at the very beginning and moving on to intermediate and advanced concepts.

Thank you for your support. I wish you all the best in learning one of tech's most useful and longstanding languages!

Scan the QR code below

Conclusion

Congratulations on making it to the end of this guide! With the information you have learned in this book, you are now able to carry out queries that range from the simplest to the most complex in RDBMS using SQL. In addition to this, know all the steps and possibilities for creating your own project with SQL and start showcasing everything you know.

In this book, you read about the basics concerning data, databases, and ANSI/SQL and the different dialects that can be used with the most popular database providers. You were taught about the basics of SQL such as its syntax, data types, and even comparison symbols that can be used in your code. Understanding this information is essential to ensure that your journey in learning SQL has the most benefits.

You have also seen some of the differences between ANSI/SQL, MySQL, PL/SQL, PL/pgSQL, and T-SQL. Remember that while you will likely learn in more depth one of these dialects, it will be essential to have a general idea of each of them in case you are exposed to databases using a dialect different from what you are used to. If you have any doubts, remember that at the end of

Chapter 3, there are three tables that contain most of the data types and the languages that support them. Use this information to your advantage.

Now that you are able to create your own projects and manage them with everything you have learned, the keyword will be: practice! Even if you are not currently using this in your workplace at the moment, the more you practice, the better you will be at writing queries. In addition to this, remember that this will also enable you to completely change professional directions if you so wish to. Data analysts are in high demand in the market and companies are always looking for people who can provide efficient and applicable data analysis.

Lastly, I wish you the best of luck in your new journey and I hope you feel motivated to continue learning and understanding SQL techniques to help you manage RDBMS you work with and create efficiently. Remember to use this as a reference guide if you need to! The information you have here can be applied to different situations and is only the beginning of the path you will trail in this area.

If you feel this book has somehow helped you, please leave a review, so other readers can know what to expect and the information available herein. Enjoy your new skills and happy SQLing!

References

Berry, E. (2021, November 17). *Understanding SQL dialects.* Arctype Blog. https://arctype.com/blog/sql-dialects/

Bipp. (n.d.). *Intermediate SQL.* https://bipp.io/sql-tutorial/intermediate-sql

Biswal, A. (2023, January 30). *What is data structure: Types, classifications and applications.* Simplilearn. https://www.simplilearn.com/tutorials/data-structure-tutorial/what-is-data-structure

Buuck, B. (2022, November 29). *Python vs. SQL: A deep dive comparison.* StreamSets. https://streamsets.com/blog/python-vs-sql/

Component Source. (n.d.). *PL/SQL developer compatibility.* https://www.componentsource.com/product/pl-sql-developer/compatibilities

Cook, A. (n.d.). *Writing efficient queries.* Kaggle. https://www.kaggle.com/code/alexisbcook/writing-efficient-queries

Crabtree, M. (2023, January). *The top 10 data analytics careers: Skills, salaries & career prospects.* Data Camp. https://www.datacamp.com/blog/top-ten-analytics-careers

dbForge Team. (2022, November 4). *Oracle data types with examples - Complete guide.* Devart Blog. https://blog.devart.com/oracle-data-types.html

Frazier, C. (2023, April 13). *How I used SQL to advance in my career.* LearnSQL.com. https://learnsql.com/blog/sql-to-advance-my-career/

Garfield, Stan. "What Are Some Inspirational Quotes about Learning or Sharing Knowledge?" Medium. Accessed November 16, 2023. https://stangarfield.medium.com/what-are-some-inspirational-quotes-about-learning-or-sharing-knowledge-856751bdea6c

GeeksforGeeks. (2023, May 10). *SQL | DDL, DQL, DML, DCL and TCL commands.* https://www.geeksforgeeks.org/sql-ddl-dql-dml-dcl-tcl-commands/?ref=lbp

IBM. (2023). *What is a relational database?* https://www.ibm.com/topics/relational-databases

Laleye, B. (2022, July 19). *Top 5 SQL challenges preventing you from mastering it.* RestApp. https://restapp.io/blog/top-5-challenges-of-using-sql/

Lenon, N. (2023, May 8). *Become a SQL expert: A comprehensive guide to database development.* Medium. https://levelup.gitconnected.com/become-a-sql-expert-a-comprehensive-guide-to-database-development-c5a53f325b21

Manoj, H. (2023, August 8). *Advantages and disadvantages of SQL?* Skill Vertex. https://www.skillvertex.com/blog/advantages-and-disadvantages-of-sql/

Mayankanand2701. (2022, November 7). *Disadvantages of using MySQL.* GeeksforGeeks. https://www.geeksforgeeks.org/disadvantages-of-using-mysql/

McNeillie, K. (2020, October). *How to become a SQL expert.* Data Camp. https://www.datacamp.com/blog/how-to-become-a-sql-expert

Microsoft Learn. (2023, July 13). *Transact-SQL reference (database engine).* https://learn.microsoft.com/en-us/sql/t-sql/language-reference?view=sql-server-ver16

Microsoft Learn. (2023, May 23). *What are the Microsoft SQL database functions?* https://learn.microsoft.com/en-us/sql/t-sql/functions/functions?view=sql-server-ver16

Mode Analytics. (n.d.). *Mode SQL tutorial.* https://mode.com/sql-tutorial/

Mode Resources. (2016, May 23). *Performance tuning SQL queries.* https://mode.com/sql-tutorial/sql-performance-tuning/

MongoDB. (n.d.). *What is a non-relational database?* https://www.mongodb.com/databases/non-relational

MySQL. (n.d.). *Chapter 11: Data types.* https://dev.mysql.com/doc/refman/8.0/en/data-types.html

Oracle Help Center. (n.d.). *Data types.* https://docs.oracle.com/en/database/oracle/oracle-database/21/sqlrf/Data-Types.html#GUID-A3C0D836-BADB-44E5-A5D4-265BA5968483

Pankaj. (2022, December 15). *SQL data types.* Digital Ocean. https://www.digitalocean.com/community/tutorials/sql-data-types#sql-date-and-time-data-types

Peck, J. (2020, June 29). *SQL vs R. Which to use for data analysis?* Dataform. https://dataform.co/blog/sql-vs-r

Pedamkar, P. (2023, July 6). *Relational database advantages.* EDUCBA. https://www.educba.com/relational-database-advantages/

Pelgrim, R. (2022, March 14). *SQL vs Python for data analysis.* Airbyte. https://airbyte.com/blog/sql-vs-python-data-analysis

Peterson, R. (2023a, July 27). *What is PostgreSQL? Introduction, history, features, advantages.* Guru99. https://www.guru99.com/introduction-postgresql.html

Peterson, R. (2023b, August 14). *What is a database? Definition, meaning, types with example.* Guru99. https://www.guru99.com/introduction-to-database-sql.html

Pijacek, R. (2019). *Microsoft SQL Server pros and cons.* LeanSQL.com. https://learnsql.com/blog/microsoft-sql-server-pros-and-cons/

PostgreSQL. (2022, February 10). *Chapter 8. Data types.* https://www.postgresql.org/docs/current/datatype.html

Saksshijain1. (2018, January 12). *SQL data types.* GeeksforGeeks. https://www.geeksforgeeks.org/sql-data-types/

Sarang S. (2023, March 6). *12 tips for optimizing SQL queries for faster performance.*

Learning SQL. https://medium.com/learning-sql/12-tips-for-optimizing-sql-queries-for-faster-performance-8c6c092d7af1

Schildorfer, F. (2021, December 17). *Data structures in SQL: The definitive guide.* Arctype Blog. https://arctype.com/blog/data-structures-in-sql/

Shin, T. (2022, December 16). *10 advanced SQL concepts you should know for data science interviews.* Built In. https://builtin.com/data-science/advanced-sql

Shivanimotarwar. (2023, January 22). *SQL vs R - Which to use for data analysis?* GeeksforGeeks. https://www.geeksforgeeks.org/sql-vs-r-which-to-use-for-data-analysis/

Shreyanshi_arun. (2018, January 17). *SQL | Creating roles.* GeeksforGeeks. https://www.geeksforgeeks.org/sql-creating-roles/?ref=lbp

Simplilearn. (2023a, March 1). *What is Transact SQL (T-SQL) and its type of functions?* https://www.simplilearn.com/tutorials/sql-tutorial/transact-sql

Simplilearn. (2023b, August 8). *Data analyst: Job description, responsibilities and skills required.* https://www.simplilearn.com/data-analyst-job-description-article

Simranjenny84. (2020, April 9). *Advantages and disadvantages of SQL.* GeeksforGeeks. https://www.geeksforgeeks.org/advantages-and-disadvantages-of-sql/

Singh, H. (2019, August 14). *Oracle database advantages, disadvantages and features [Guide 2023].* The NineHertz. https://theninehertz.com/blog/advantages-of-using-oracle-database

Sullivan, D. (2015). *Advantages & disadvantages of Oracle SQL.* Techwalla. https://www.techwalla.com/articles/advantages-disadvantages-of-oracle-sql

Talend. (n.d.). *SQL vs NoSQL: Differences, databases, and decisions.* https://www.talend.com/resources/sql-vs-nosql/

Talend. (2023). *What is MySQL? Everything you need to know.* https://www.talend.com/resources/what-is-mysql/

Taylor, P. (2023, September). *Ranking of the most popular database management systems worldwide, as of September 2023.* Statista. https://www.statista.com/statistics/809750/worldwide-popularity-ranking-database-management-systems/

Techstrikers. (2019). *MySQL advantages and disadvantages.* https://www.techstrikers.com/MySQL/advantages-and-disadvantages-of-mysql.php

Techstrickers. (n.d.). *MySQL features.* https://www.techstrikers.com/MySQL/mysql-features.php

Thakur, S. (2022, November 1). *Advantages and disadvantages of SQL: A popular choice for databases!* Unstop. https://unstop.com/blog/advantages-and-disadvantages-of-sql

Thornhill, J. (2022, December 6). *The future of SQL.* LearnSQL.com. https://learnsql.com/blog/future-of-sql/

Tutorials Point. (2019). *SQL - Overview*. https://www.tutorialspoint.com/sql/sql-overview.htm

Tutorials Point. (n.d.-a). *PL/SQL - Quick guide*. https://www.tutorialspoint.com/plsql/plsql_quick_guide.htm

Tutorials Point. (n.d.-b). *SQL - Syntax*. https://www.tutorialspoint.com/sql/sql-syntax.htm

Udell, A. (2022, February 9). *A quick guide to the dialects of SQL*. Medium. https://towardsdatascience.com/a-quick-guide-to-the-dialects-of-sql-7249125f9228

Vinsys. (2022, November 17). *What is advanced SQL?* https://www.vinsys.com/blog/advanced-sql-concept/

W3Schools. (n.d.). *MySQL advantages and disadvantages*. https://www.w3schools.blog/mysql-advantages-disadvantages

W3Schools. (2019). *SQL syntax*. https://www.w3schools.com/SQl/sql_syntax.asp

Wesley, D. (2023, May 14). *Is SQL still relevant?* Sursumcorda Resource Group. https://www.srgsoftware.io/blog/is-sql-still-relevant

Made in the USA
Coppell, TX
29 November 2024

41147842R00105